Terror in the Microworld

A burst of protons fills the tube. It's like being in a tunnel filled with balloons or bouncing oranges.

Slowly pushing toward you through the jiggling group of protons is a dark, strange-looking particle. It has four tentacles, sort of like arms and legs. *The intruder!*

The mysterious figure is wearing a hood-like mask, and you can't see his face. But around his waist you can see the glint of the stolen Shrinkatron belt.

"He's here," you whisper into your wrist monitor. "And he's coming closer! What should I do?"

EXPLORER™
Adventure on the Frontiers of Science.
#1

JOURNEY TO THE CENTER OF THE ATOM!

Carol Gaskin

Illustrated by
Walter P. Martishius

A Byron Preiss
Visual Publications, Inc., Book

Scholastic Inc.
New York Toronto London Auckland Sydney

Special thanks to Jean Feiwel, Greg Holch, Regina Griffin,
and Bruce Stevenson.

Book design by Alex Jay
Cover painting by Paul Rivoche
Cover design by Alex Jay
Mechanicals by Mary LeCleir

Editor: Ruth Ashby

Scholastic Books are available at special discounts for quantity purchases for use as premiums, promotional items, retail sales through specialty market outlets, etc. For details contact: Special Sales Manager, Scholastic Inc., 730 Broadway, New York, NY 10003.

No part of this publication may be reproduced in whole or in part, or stored in a retrieval system, or transmitted in any form or by any means, electronic, mechanical, photocopying, recording, or otherwise, without written permission of the publisher. For information regarding permission, write to Scholastic Inc., 730 Broadway, New York, NY 10003.

ISBN 0-590-40336-2

Copyright © 1987 by Byron Preiss Visual Publications, Inc.
All rights reserved. Published by Scholastic Inc.

"Explorer" is a trademark of
Byron Preiss Visual Publications, Inc.

12 11 10 9 8 7 6 5 4 3 2 1   7 8 9/8 0 1 2/9

Printed in the U.S.A.

First Scholastic printing, May 1987

THE COUNTDOWN BEGINS...

You are an explorer. You journey to places no one has ever been and face dangers no one has ever known.

Now you have a new assignment. In a moment you'll be given a briefing and will meet some of the other members of your team. At your disposal you will have the latest in scientific knowledge and technology.

Despite these advantages, at times you and your team may be exposed to extreme peril. Only the decisions you make will enable you to survive.

Are you willing to accept the risks? The choice is up to you.

■ *When you're ready, turn the page.*

PROJECT SUMMARY

Your assignment: You will journey to the center of the atom to find the smallest particle of matter known to science.

You will be joining a team of physicists as they probe for the key to the universe.

We know that everything in the universe is made of tiny particles called atoms. But what are atoms made of? Scientists have identified many "subatomic" particles — particles that are smaller than atoms. They have named the smallest, most basic of these a *quark*. But no one has ever seen a quark. Some scientists are not even sure that quarks exist.

After years of work, a brilliant inventor has created a device that will allow him to enter the subatomic world. The project is Top Secret — but the excitement in the laboratory is hard to hide!

You have been chosen to assist the inventor as he tests his new device. You must discover the truth: Do quarks exist? What is the universe really made of?

■ *The following Personnel Dossiers and Equipment Report contain orientation material that will help you on your journey to the microworld. If you prefer to go directly to the lab to meet your team members, turn to page 1.*

PERSONNEL DOSSIERS

Your team consists of two of the world's top scientists.

PROFESSOR GRACE PARTON, Particle Physicist

Born: May 23, 1946; Omaha, Nebraska

Educ.: Ph.D., Anderson Institute, 1973; Full professorship, Sternford, 1980

Awards: Keeler Prize for Excellence in High Energy Physics, 1983; International Organization for Subnuclear Research Chair at World Science Caucus, 1984–5; Private grants for research on quark model, 1986

Remarks: Professor Parton is a patient teacher and thorough researcher with an IQ well into the genius range. She has a great love of chemistry and physics and a driving curiosity. She has a particular talent for deducing cause and effect.

She is known to be prudent, cautious, tidy, and organized. She enjoys music, architecture, and mathematics, and finds satisfaction in having all things in their proper place.

Prof. Parton will monitor the team from the lab, direct all tests and experiments, and operate the accelerator. She will be in constant contact with you and your teammate, Dr. Maxwell.

PERSONNEL DOSSIERS

DR. HOWARD MAXWELL, inventor of the Decimetric Shrinkatron and programmer of Elwat

Born: October 27, 1957; Nome, Alaska

Educ.: Ph.D., University of Tokyo, 1982

Credits: Holds 147 patents, the first awarded at the age of 14.

Remarks: You will be accompanying Dr. Maxwell as he tests his new invention. Dr. Maxwell is generally regarded as a brilliant inventor and computer programmer. He is known for his sense of humor — Elwat, his computer, is short for "Elementary, Watson" — and for his problem-solving ability.

He is adventurous and a risk-taker, but has been known to be rash and lacking in foresight.

He is likely to make leaps of instinct rather than logic. His favorite projects are those that range "from the sublime to the ridiculous," as he puts it.

He is an amateur chef — he enjoys anything that entails combining ingredients in untried ways — but his culinary creations occasionally backfire. We recommend you avoid his cooking.

EQUIPMENT REPORT

DECIMETRIC SHRINKATRON: Compact belt attachment. This device, the invention of Dr. Howard Maxwell, will allow you to reduce your physical size in meters by powers of 10. There are only two such devices in existence. Both have been successfully tested from 10^0 to 10^{-3}, one factor at a time. The full range and capacities of the instrument are untested.

POWER BOOSTER: You will be supplied with a totally untested electronic device that is designed to accelerate you by MeV's (millions of electron volts.) Caution: Use special care with antigravity setting.

ELWAT: 14-megabyte DRAM computer. A natural-language, voice recognition, multitasking data retrieval system, programmed and designed by Dr. Maxwell. You will be able to access all relevant charts, tables, diagrams, calculations, projections, and scientific data.

VIDEO/COMPUTER WRIST MONITOR: A minielectronic device with which you will be able to communicate with Elwat and your team back at the lab.

■ *End orientation material. If you want more information on the world of the atom, turn to page 112.*

■ *If you are ready to begin your assignment now, turn to page 1.*

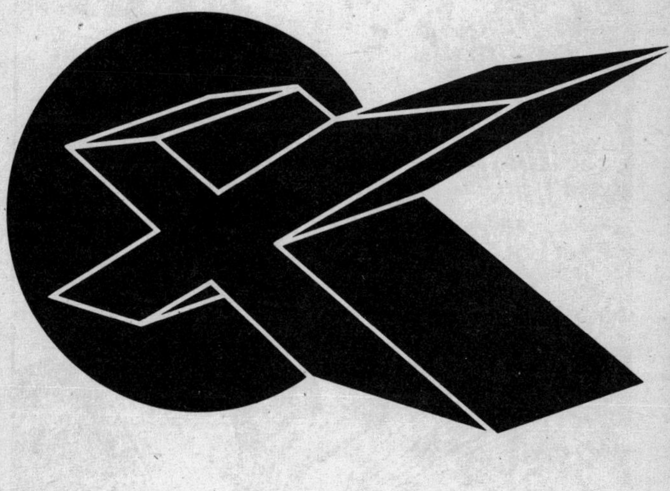

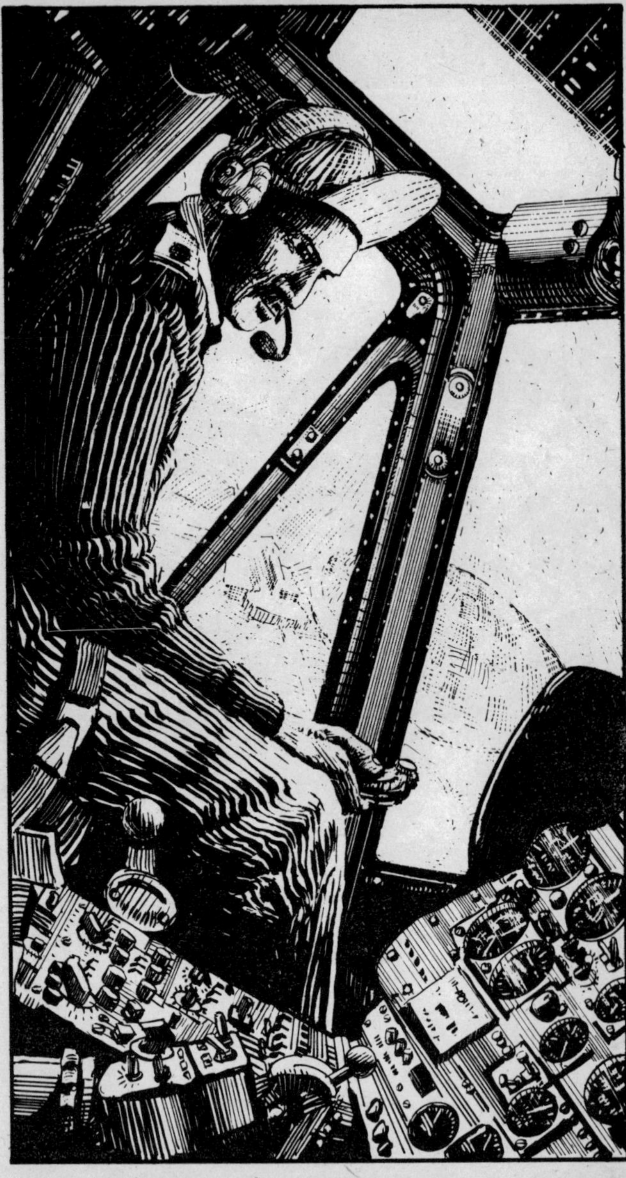

1

Your helicopter hovers above one of the strangest buildings you have ever seen. It's a huge narrow ring, miles across, encircling acres of patchwork farmland. From the air it looks like something ancient spacemen left here thousands of years ago.

"That's the circular accelerator," says the pilot as he maneuvers the chopper onto a tiny landing strip. "And here's the lab."

You climb down next to a cluster of buildings connected to one side of the ring. A door swings open and you can see two figures in white jumpsuits.

The pilot flashes you a thumbs-up sign as you push your way to the door through the gale-force wind made by the rising chopper.

A plump young man with glasses and a mustache greets you eagerly.

"Come in, come in," he says. "I'm Howard Maxwell — 'Max' to my friends. We've been waiting for you. We can hardly wait

2

to get started." He grabs your hand and pulls you down a long corridor.

The woman beside him drags him back by his sleeve. Her hair is as white as her jumpsuit, and her eyes are a bright, twinkly blue.

"You're always in such a hurry, Max," she says, extending her hand to you. "I'm Grace Parton. How do you do."

You are ushered into an enormous laboratory. The room is lined with blinking computer banks, flashing video screens, and clacking printers.

Max gestures proudly at a computer monitor and keyboard.

"Meet Elwat," he says. "It's short for 'Elementary, Watson.' Elwat is our computer, and the last member of our team."

You type "HELLO, ELWAT."

"WELCOME," replies the computer. Its voice sounds like a squeaky, digitalized version of Max's. "LET'S GO."

"That's my Elwat!" beams Max.

Prof. Parton hands you a special Shrinkatron suit. Then she fastens a belt around your waist. Attached to the belt is a little black box with several switches and dials. The Decimetric Shrinkatron!

"These little wonders are our tickets to the microworld," says Max, buckling a similar belt around his own generous waistline. "The Shrinkatron measures in meters — a meter is about three feet — and will decrease your size by powers of 10, one jump at a time. We'll be starting at 10^0, or one meter."

"Do you understand exponential notation?" asks Prof. Parton. "Powers of 10?"

"My exponential notation is a little rusty," you admit.

"Well, then, let's ask Elwat for a chart," says Max.

■ *Ask Elwat for a chart explaining powers of 10. Turn to page 7.*

4

The hand is reaching for you. You decide you'd better hide, and dash down a corridor between two books. Then you slide under a loose sheet of paper and hold your breath.

Piles of books are sliding across the counter like crumbling mountains as the giant hand makes its search. Suddenly your shelter of paper is ripped away and the hand closes over you. You are trapped in a cage of fingers!

"Don't worry, it's *me*," booms a faraway voice. You notice that the cuff circling the hand is white, like your own jumpsuit. And one of the fingers is wearing a pretty pearly ring. It's Prof. Parton!

"Now try your wrist monitor," the voice says. The hand moves away. Two anxious faces appear on the video screen. Max and Prof. Parton!

"You're all right!" you say, relieved. "What happened?"

"A man in a ski mask and dark clothes burst into the lab," says Prof. Parton.

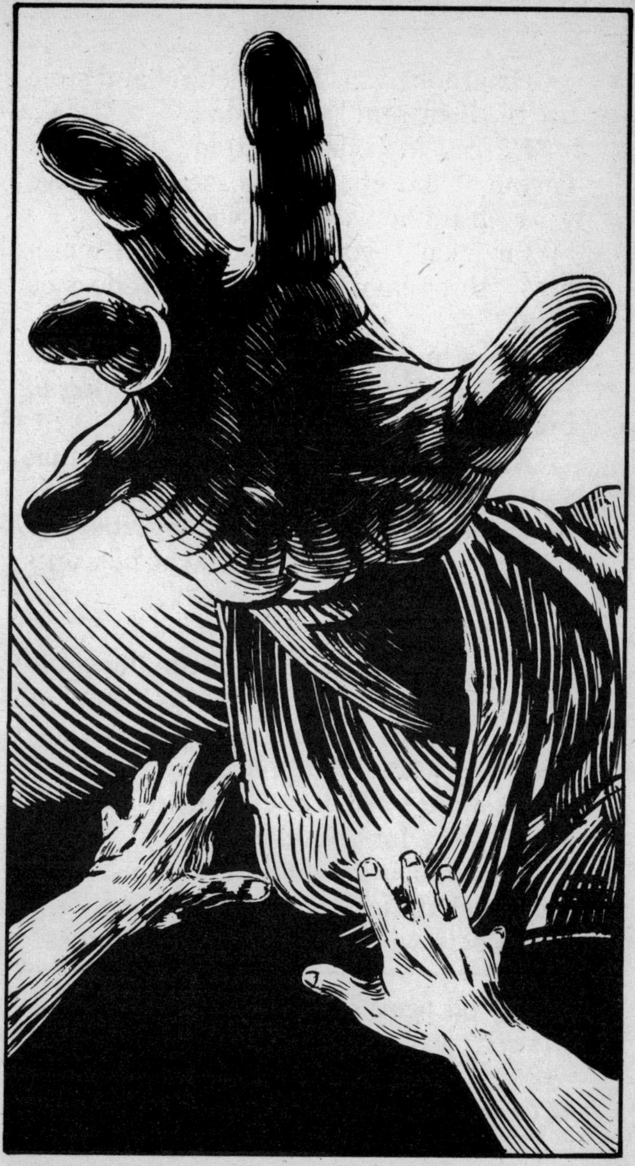

6

"He grabbed me from behind and stole my Shrinkatron!" wails Max.

"He ran in your direction," says Prof. Parton, "and then he disappeared. We were afraid he was after *you*."

"I'm okay," you tell your team members. "But who was he? And what does he want?"

"We're not sure," answers Max. "But Elwat says that someone's been trying to break into the computer lately."

"And our night watchman says that someone has been snooping around the accelerator," adds Prof. Parton. "It seems we have a subatomic spy! Maybe he wants to be the first to find a quark!"

"Not if I can help it!" you say.

"If he's used the Shrinkatron, he could be anywhere by now," says Max. "But I've sealed all the exits, and I'm going to stay here to search the lab. Are you willing to go on alone? We'll ask Elwat to pick the safest place for you to shrink."

"Or you could wait here with us, while we search the lab," says Prof. Parton. "You could help with the nooks and crannies."

■ *Do you want to keep shrinking by yourself? Turn to page 23.*

■ *Or would you rather join in the search for the intruder? Turn to page 10.*

"We've chosen to use meters because they are based on units of ten, rather than units of twelve like feet," explains Dr. Parton. "And we use exponents to write very large or very small numbers."

"If you multiply the number ten by itself," says Max, "you have ten times ten, or ten to the second power." He punches Elwat's keyboard. You read:

$10^2 = 10 \times 10 = 100$. PLEASE NOTE

THAT 100 HAS TWO ZEROS.

"The little numeral 'two' written above the ten is called an 'exponent,'" says Max. "Now let's do ten to the third power."

But Elwat has already spun out a column of numbers:

$10^3 = 10 \times 10 \times 10 = 1,000$ THREE ZEROS.

$10^4 = 10 \times 10 \times 10 \times 10 = 10,000$ FOUR ZEROS.
$10^5 = 10 \times 10 \times 10 \times 10 \times 10 = 100,000$ FIVE ZEROS.
$10^6 = 1,000,000 = 1$ million SIX ZEROS.
$10^{12} = 1,000,000,000,000 = 1$ trillion TWELVE ZEROS.

"Whoah!" says Max. "Thanks, Elwat!"
"Show us what happens when we *divide* by ten," suggests Prof. Parton. "Then we write negative exponents."
Elwat whirs into action. You read:

$10^1 = 10$
$10^0 = 10 \div 10 = 1$
$10^{-1} = 10 \div 100 = 0.1$, or one tenth
$10^{-2} = 10 \div 1,000 = 0.01$, or one hundredth
$10^{-3} = 10 \div 10,000 = 0.001$, or one thousandth
$10^{-6} = 10 \div 10,000,000 = 0.000001$, or one millionth

"A millionth of a meter is called a 'micron,'" Max tells you. "We'll be shrinking even smaller than that! Atoms are so tiny, we measure them in 'angstrom units' — one angstrom is 10^{-10} meters. There are about 254 million angstroms to an inch. But you can learn as we go along. Are you ready?"

"Wait!" says Prof. Parton. "Maybe you'd like a tour of the accelerator first? There's so much to teach you about subatomic particles!"

■ *Are you ready to test the Shrinkatron with Max? Turn to page 19.*

■ *Do you want to tour the accelerator with Prof. Parton? Turn to page 13.*

You decide to join in the search for the intruder. There are certain advantages to being four inches tall!

"Put me on the floor," you tell your teammates. "The last time I saw the guy he was running this way."

Prof. Parton lifts you gently to the floor. "Stay close to the wall," she says. "We don't want to step on you!"

The black and white tiled floor stretches away like a giant's checkerboard. The countertop could be the roof of a five-story building. And the blinking lights on the computer banks look like distant towers, warning low-flying planes of dangers in the night.

You feel as if you are in a strange, deserted city, surrounded by steel skyscrapers and threatening shadows.

You look toward the horizon, where the wall ends at a corner. Something is moving!

"I think I see him," you say into your wrist monitor. "In the corner — wait, I

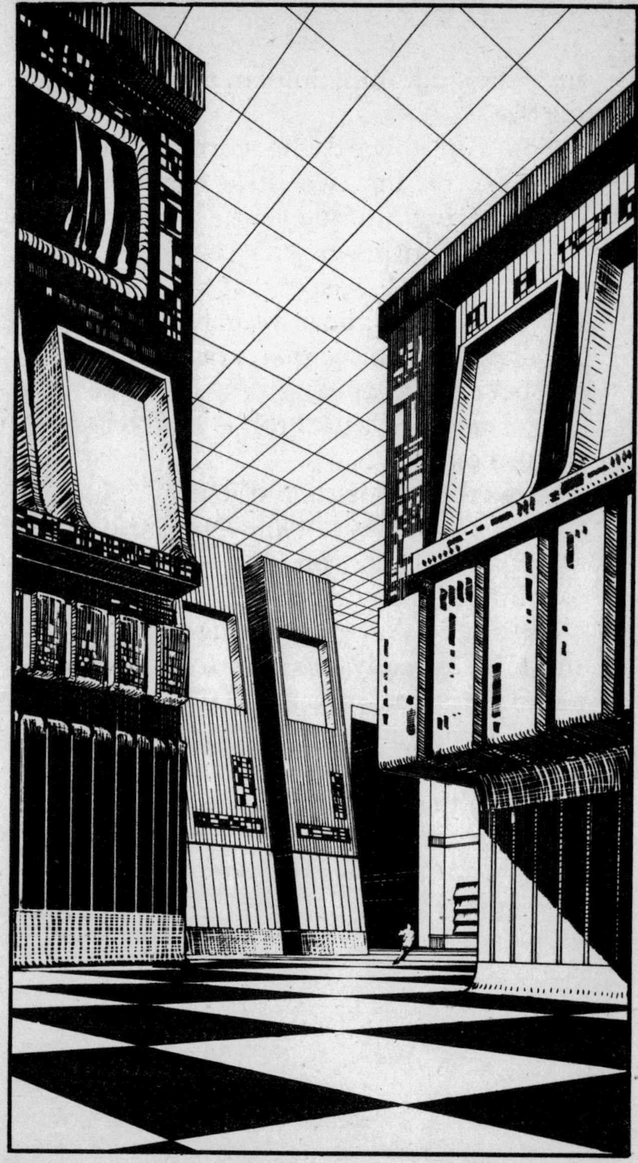

12

think he's climbing into an air conditioning vent!"

You run toward the corner, keeping your eye on the two little feet that are disappearing into the vent.

Max is waiting by the vent when you reach it. The lowest metal slat covering the vent is just above your head. Behind the slat, you can see that a piece of screen has been pried up.

You check in with Prof. Parton on your wrist monitor.

"Max thinks you should go in after him," she says. "He may not know that you have a second Shrinkatron, and you could follow him at a distance.

"But it could be very dangerous. And I think it's already too late. If he's shrunk again, he is small enough to ride anywhere in the building on an air current."

"Tell Max I'm ready to try," you say. "If I don't see him, I'll come out."

■ *Climb into the air conditioning vent. Turn to page 17.*

13

You decide to learn more about the microworld before you shrink to microsize.

Prof. Parton guides you through the accelerator facility. You enter a tunnel that has a metal tube running its entire length.

"The tunnel goes on for miles," explains Prof. Parton. "It's the ring you saw from the sky. We shoot a beam of protons into orbit in the tube. We can direct the beam from the lab.

"Protons are subject to electromagnetic force, so we can boost their speed by activating stronger and stronger electromagnets at various points in the tube.

"The faster a particle goes, the more its energy increases. Finally, we direct the beam at a target and the protons collide with other particles. These high energy collisions produce many types of smaller particles that are not visible, even with our most powerful microscopes."

14

"But if you can't see them," you ask, "how do you know they are there?"

"I was getting to that," says Prof. Parton. "Some of the particles pass into a collecting device we call a bubble chamber. Here it is."

You are standing next to an enormous metal contraption, several stories high.

"You certainly need huge machines to study tiny particles," you comment.

"The particles are tiny but the *energies* are huge, so we need big machines," Prof. Parton answers.

"But you can't see through metal," you say. "How does it work?"

"The bubble chamber is filled with liquid," answers Prof. Parton. "It is heated almost to the boiling point, but kept under pressure so it doesn't boil. When the particles enter the chamber, the pressure is released. As the liquid starts to boil, the particles leave trails of tiny bubbles as they speed through the chamber. These tracks are photographed. We can't see the particles, but we can see where they've been."

Prof. Parton shows you a handful of bubble track photographs. They look to you like strings of bubbles — just straight lines, spirals, and clusters of bubbles on a black background.

"We can only tell what kinds of particles

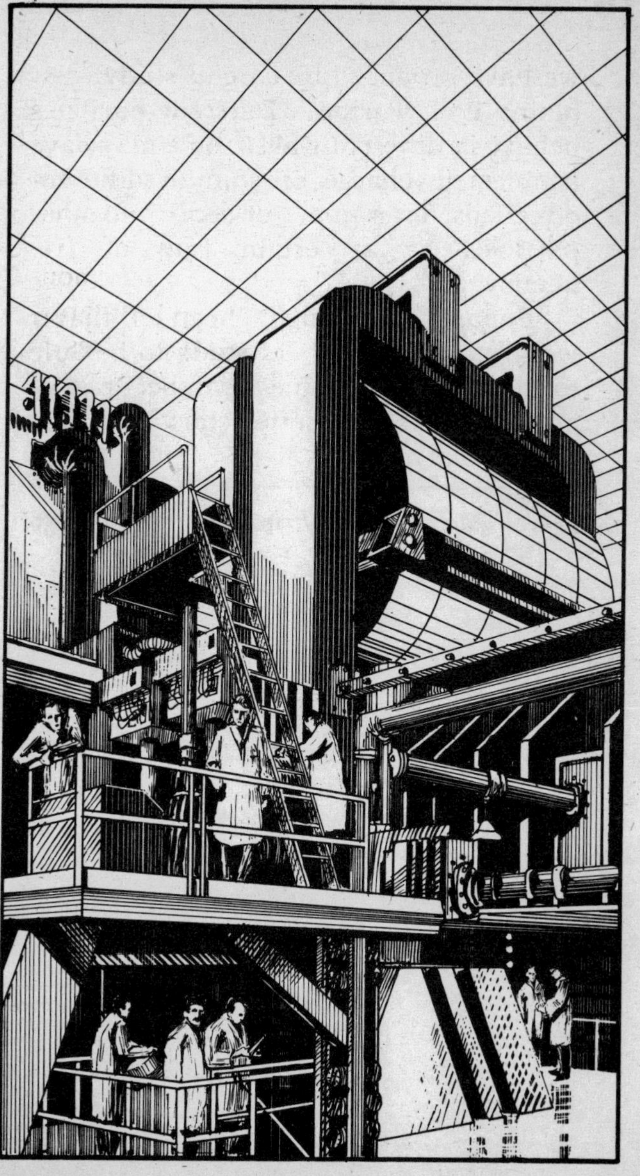

16

we have produced by careful study," explains Prof. Parton. "Different particles behave in different ways. Some may have an electric charge or spin in different directions, for example, or decay into other particles at a certain rate of frequency...."

"Enough!" you laugh. "I can tell that it would take me years of study to be able to decipher a bubble chamber photograph. I guess I'd better start shrinking and see for myself!"

■ *Get ready to start shrinking. Turn to page 19.*

17

Accepting a boost from Max, you crawl behind the metal slat that covers the air conditioning vent. Then you squeeze past the torn piece of screen that serves as a filter, and enter a huge metal duct.

The duct is dark and hollow. It goes on for as far as you can see, which isn't far.

"Can you shine a light in here?" you whisper into your wrist monitor.

"Max is on his way," Prof. Parton whispers back. "Be careful!"

You flatten yourself against the wall of the duct. Suddenly the tunnel is flooded with bright stripes of light. Max is shining a flashlight through the slats on the vent.

A dark figure is cowering in one of the light spots. He leaps to his feet and springs into the next strip of shadow.

"I see him!" you hiss excitedly. "But I don't think he can see me. He's just my size!"

The figure detaches itself from the

18

shadow and darts into the next strip of darkness.

You don't want to alert him. But you'll have to hurry if you want to catch him before he can shrink again.

■ *Do you want to chase him? Turn to page 26.*

■ *Do you want to grow back to 10^0 and try to block his path? Turn to page 29.*

You decide you're ready to start shrinking.

"This is it!" says Max. "Strap on your wrist monitor. You'll be able to talk to the lab, and also communicate with Elwat."

You buckle the miniature computer/video screen to your wrist. Max bustles excitedly around the lab as Prof. Parton sits in front of Elwat.

"You'll go first," says Max. "We want to monitor your first move from here. Now remember, you can only shrink by one power of 10 at a time. You'll be starting at 10^0, or about one meter. Not much smaller than your normal size. Here, I'll show you. Don't worry — it doesn't hurt a bit."

Max sets a dial at your waist to zero. Then he pushes a red button to activate the Shrinkatron.

You feel an itchy, bubbly sensation, as though your body is fizzing like a newly opened bottle of soda pop. It passes quickly. You are about three feet tall.

"That was easy!" you say.

"Great!" he answers. "Now sit on this counter and set the dial for minus one. After you shrink, test your wrist monitor. You should be tuned to Professor Parton, right here in the lab. Then wait for me to join you."

You sit on a counter that's been built against the wall and turn to -1. Then you press the red button. Your body tickles all over.

You're standing on the counter in the lab, surrounded by gigantic books, seas of paper, and mountains of measuring tools. At 10^{-1} meters, or 10 centimeters, you're only about four inches tall!

It's hard to see beyond the books and papers, but there seems to be some kind of hubbub in the lab. You hear thunderous noises and shouting. You've forgotten to activate your wrist monitor!

You switch on the little screen and wait for Prof. Parton's face to come into focus. She is screaming!

Climbing up onto a pile of books, you scan the lab. A dark figure is running toward you. He has Max's Shrinkatron!

"Max! Professor Parton!" you call into your wrist monitor. But the screen on your wrist is blank.

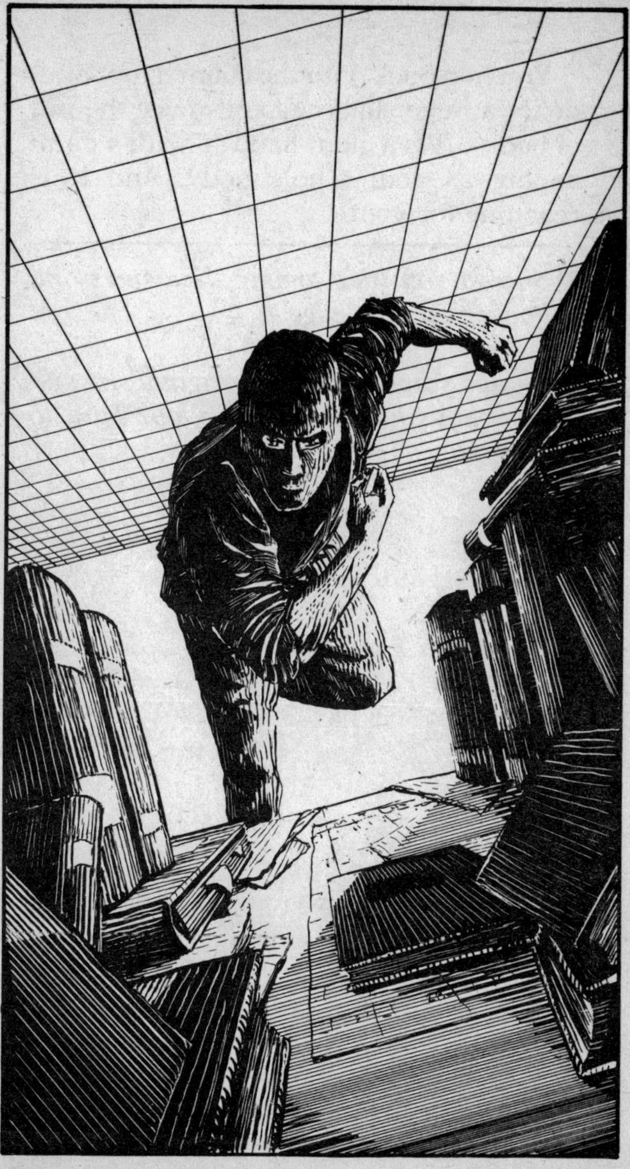

22

You hop back onto the countertop. Suddenly a huge shadow looms over the hill of books. It is a giant hand — with a palm as big as your whole body. And it is reaching for you!

- ■ *Should you hide among the papers and books? Turn to page 4.*

- ■ *Should you resume your original size and see what's happened in the lab? Turn to page 36.*

While you continue to explore the microworld, Prof. Parton and Max will stay in the lab in case the intruder returns.

"Where *is* the safest place to search for a quark?" you ask your teammates.

"Elwat can tell you that," says Max. You address your question to the computer.

"TRY THE TERRARIUM," Elwat answers.

"What a good idea," says Prof. Parton. She carries you to a table and sets you down next to a large glass fish tank that has been planted with ferns and mosses. From your height of four inches, it looks like a wild jungle.

"This way we'll always know where you are, no matter how much you shrink," says Max.

"Climb onto my hand if you're ready," says Prof. Parton, "and I'll put you down inside." She lowers you slowly into the lush green world of the terrarium.

"Here I go!" you say into your wrist monitor. Max's wistful face fills the little screen. You know he wishes he could go with you.

24

Setting the Shrinkatron for 10^{-2}, you push the red button and wait. A shiver later you are one centimeter tall — less than half an inch!

You are still standing on Prof. Parton's fingertip. It looks as if someone has been raking spiral patterns in reddish earth. But you know you are just looking at the whorls and ridges that make up her fingerprint. You hop to the ground as Prof. Parton's hand recedes into the sky.

The terrarium looks like a tropical forest gone mad. Towering, feathery ferns dust the sky green. Tendrils curve and spore sacs pop. Everything is moist and dripping, and it smells like a garden after a rainstorm.

You push your way through a field of moss that comes up to your shoulders. It's rough going, and in no time you are perspiring. You stop to admire the underside of a mushroom. Its arching ribs are as remote and delicate as a cathedral ceiling.

A deafening buzz interrupts your reverie. It sounds as if a helicopter is about to land on your head. It's a mosquito, and it's as big as you!

■ *Do you want to battle the mosquito? Turn to page 43.*

■ *Do you want to shrink to 10^{-3}? Turn to page 45.*

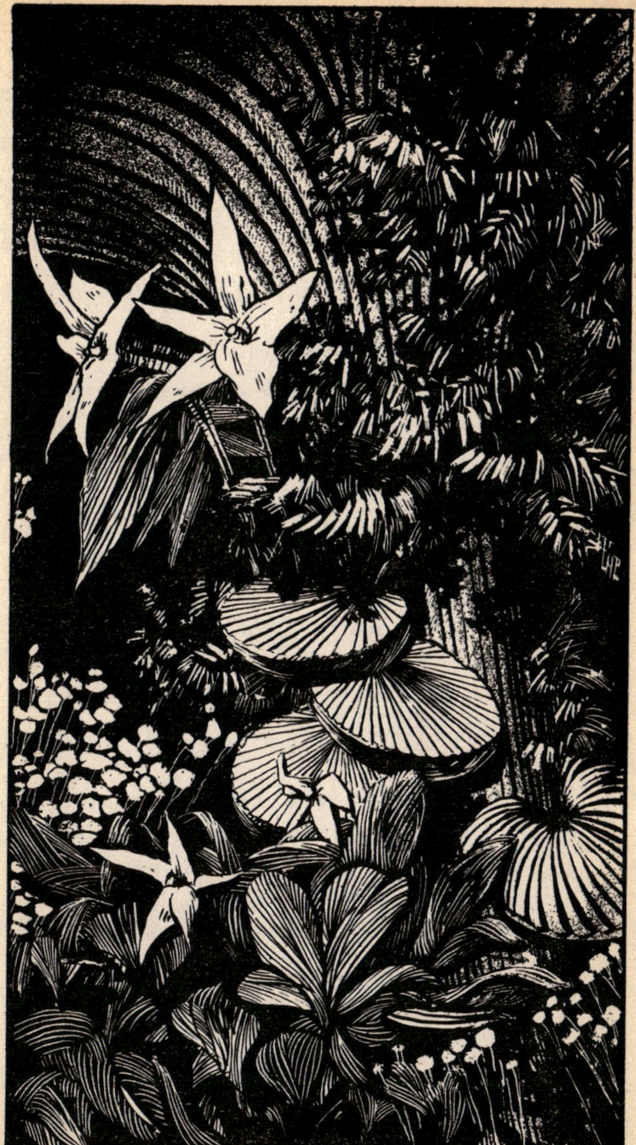

26

You decide to chase him.

The intruder steps into a strip of light and so do you. Then you both slip into the safety of darkness. So far so good. You don't think he's seen you.

There he is again. You move as he moves, hurrying through the light and resting in the shadow. But at this rate, you'll never gain on him. You decide to try to speed through two stripes of light for his one.

You see him and run. Light, dark, light, dark — *freeze*.

Only four stripes of light separate you now. You are breathing heavily. Suddenly the intruder breaks free of the shadows.

"*Eeeh*, hee hee," he cackles shrilly, "you'll *never* catch me!"

The chase is on. You make a dash for the mocking figure.

Light, dark, light, dark — the intruder seems to be moving in slow motion, as if in a strobe light. And then all at once he is gone!

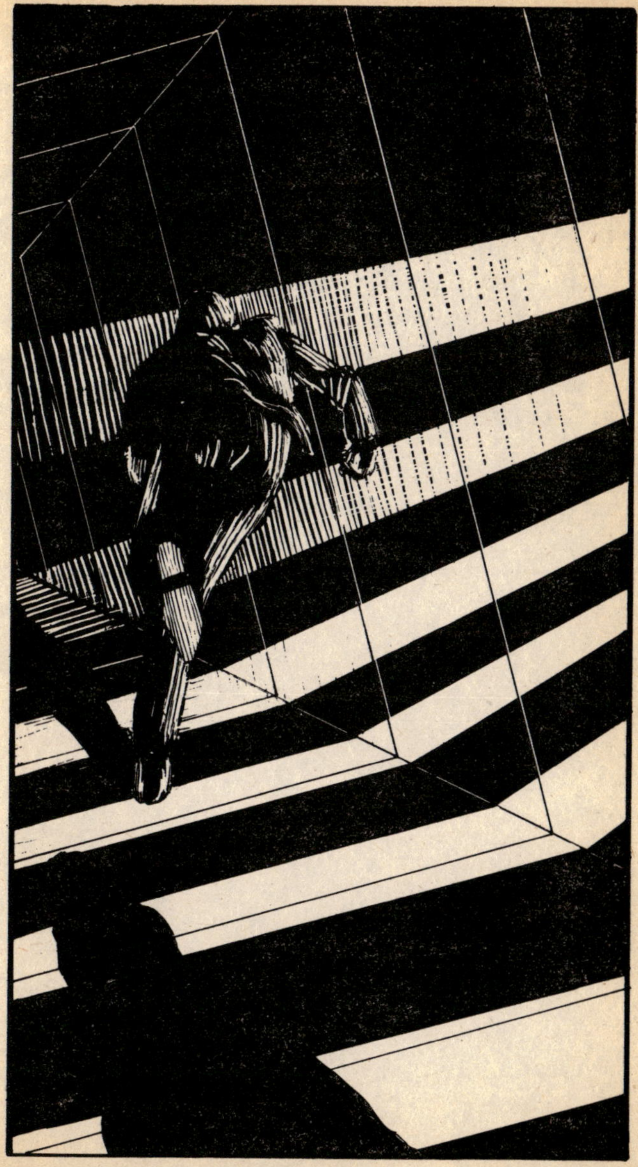

28

You run to the spot where you saw him vanish. But he's already too tiny to be seen with the naked eye.

"I lost him," you say into the wrist monitor. "He shrank."

"Good try," says Max. "Come on back, and we'll send you on your way to the real microworld."

■ *Resume your search for a quark. Turn to page 23.*

You decide to try to block the intruder's path. All you have to do is grow! Then you can grab him.

Setting the Shrinkatron back to 10^0, you press the red button.

This time you feel some pain. You are jammed inside an air conditioning vent, and can hardly move! Your arms are trapped at your sides, and your knees won't bend.

Something climbs across your chest and grabs the collar of your jumpsuit. It is a tiny man, all dressed in black. He is so close you are almost cross-eyed, and you can't quite make out his face. But you can hear his squeaky giggling, like the buzzing of a fly.

The man climbs up the side of your cheek and creeps through your hair like a spider. You try shaking your head, but he won't come loose. It *itches*. You can't scratch.

The crablike crawling nears your ear. He's climbing inside!

30

"Get out of my ear!" you scream.

"*Heeee!* Hee hee!" The intruder's giggling is unbearable. He's beating a rhythm on your eardrum and singing the television jingle you hate the most.

"I'll never leave unless you give up this project," he tells you. "No matter how much you shrink or grow, I'll stay right here in your ear."

"*Buzzzz, hummm,* dum de deedle dum. . . ." The noises and chatter, singing and itching, wheedling and needling, are driving you crazy. After 17 hours you resign from the project and go into writing television commercials full-time.

THE END

You decide to return to your teammates as fast as you can. You can still hear the siren wailing in the lab.

"I'm starting to grow," you say as you adjust the Shrinkatron and hit the red button.

You are growing in stages, 10^{-13}, 10^{-12}, but you are still inside the hydrogen atom. You are feeling okay.

10^{-11}, 10^{-10}, *whoah!* Something is happening! You are expanding out of control! *Zooooosh!* You are spinning, whirling, telescoping faster than you can think! Your body feels like a rocket hurtling through space. You see flashes of black, white, black, white.... Suddenly *everything* goes black.

You return to consciousness in the emptiness and silence of space. Your body shrieks with pain, but at least you are sure you are awake.

"Help!" you cry into your wrist monitor. "I can hardly breathe! I don't know

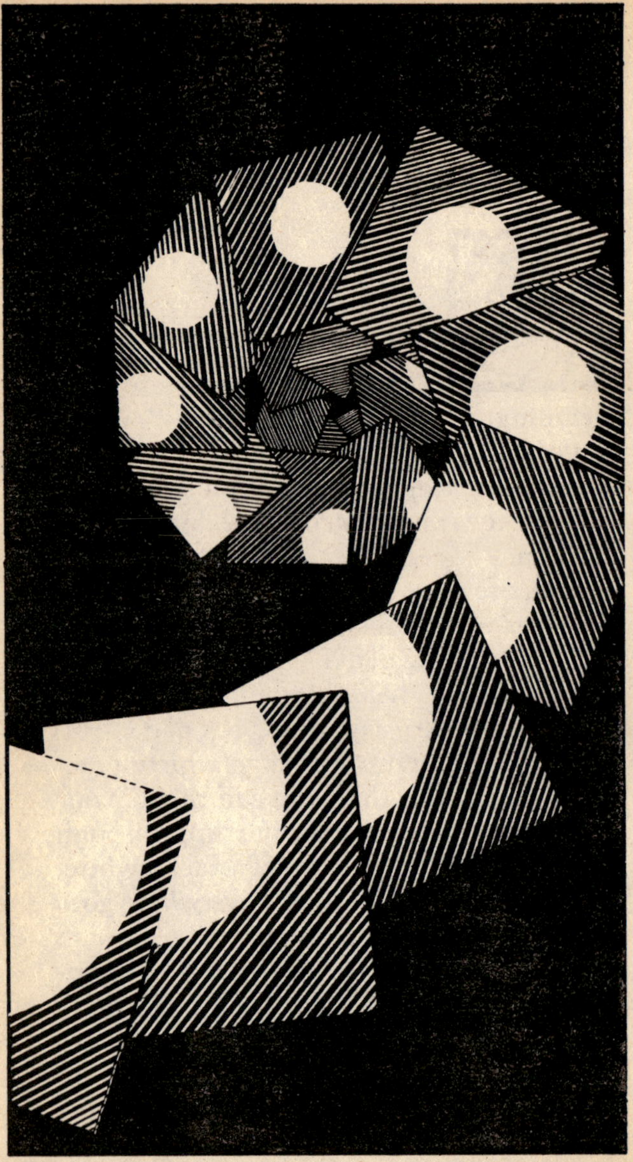

what's happening! I have cramps in my stomach!"

"It sounds as if you have the bends," says Max. "Just take it easy and look around you." His voice sounds tiny and very far away. "Where are you now?"

"I don't know," you gasp. "Maybe I'm still in an electron cloud. It looks like outer space. I can see tiny flecks of light, like stars. But wait — there is something in the distance. I think it's the moon! No, it's the *earth!* It looks just like the pictures I've seen from NASA!"

"It sounds like you're really in space!" says Max. "You must have hit the antigravity setting on the power booster at the same time you hit the Shrinkatron button. From what you describe, I'd say you're about one hundred thousand kilometers away!"

You check the power booster on your belt. Sure enough, one of the dials reads "POSITIVE GRAVITY."

"It looks like you're right, Max," you say. "But what size am I? And what do I do now?"

"You'll have to stay put for a few moments until you catch your breath," says

Max. "Have the cramps in your stomach slowed down?"

"I'm all right now," you answer. "They've passed. It's glorious out here — the sight is indescribable."

"Well, I guess we've tested the limits of the Shrinkatron!" says Max. "But I still don't think you should move for a bit. Maybe you'll spot some particles in space. They're out there, you know. Particles bombard the earth in the form of cosmic rays."

"What do you think would happen if I started to shrink from here?" you ask. "Do you suppose I could find quarks in space?"

"I have no idea," says Max. "If it worked, you could return to the lab a superhero. But it sounds too dangerous, even for me. You would have to shrink again from there. We know how far away you are, but we don't know how *big* you are. What does the dial on the Shrinkatron say?"

You check the dial on your belt.

"It says 10^0!" you report. "I'm back to three feet tall!"

"I think you should try to reverse the process," says Max. "Leave the Shrinkatron set to 10^0, aim for Earth, move the dial on the power booster to POSITIVE GRAVITY, and power-boost yourself back to Earth!"

■ *Do you want to follow Max's advice? Turn to page 71.*

■ *Do you want to risk shrinking in space to search for a quark? Turn to page 69.*

36

Something has obviously gone wrong. You decide to grow back to your normal size and see if you can help.

You set the dial for 10^0 and push the red button. Your body shivers pleasantly, and you're one meter tall again.

But you don't waste time trying to get back to your exact size. Max is lying on the floor of the lab! And Prof. Parton is bending over him, holding his head!

"What happened?" you cry, running to your teammates.

"A man dressed in black broke into the lab," says Prof. Parton. "He grabbed Max from behind and stole the Shrinkatron belt!"

"Who was he? What does he want?" you ask.

"We're not sure," says Prof. Parton. "But we have had some trouble lately. Elwat has been complaining that someone is trying to break into his circuits. And I think someone has been tampering with

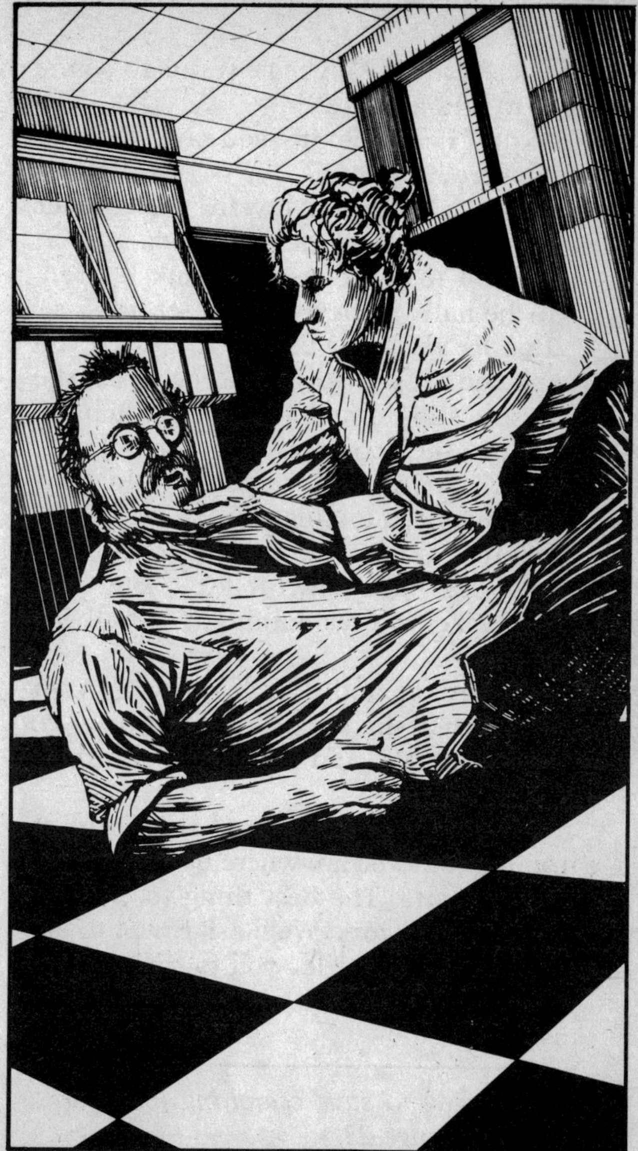

the accelerator. Maybe he wants to be the first to find a quark!"

"Not if I can help it!" you say. "Did you see where he went?"

Prof. Parton points toward the counter you were on. Past the counter is a door. You rush to the door and yank it open. But the hallway beyond is deserted.

Just as you are pushing it closed, you think you see something scurry across the floor and slip through the crack. You blink and open the door again, but see nothing. Was it a mouse? A spider? Could your eyes have been fooling you?

What if it was the intruder? Quickly, you shrink back down to 10^{-1}. But even at this size, you see nothing. The hallway is empty.

Max groans and rubs his head. "What a headache!" he says. "You'll have to go on without me, and I'll talk to you from the lab."

"If the intruder has used the Shrinkatron, he could be anywhere by now," says Prof. Parton. "The best thing to do is to continue our work. We'll ask Elwat to tell us the safest place for you to shrink."

"I'll do my best," you tell your teammates.

■ *Get ready to start searching for quarks. Turn to page 23.*

You set the Shrinkatron for 10^{-12} meters and push the red button. Once again, you feel as if there are tiny little bubbles bursting all over your body.

"I see the nucleus!" you call into your wrist monitor. "There's a tiny globe in the distance. Why, it's no bigger than a pea!"

"Keep going," Max says excitedly. "Shrink to 10^{-13}!"

You set the Shrinkatron once again. A goosefleshy feeling ripples across your skin.

"It's there!" you say. "It's sort of fuzzy, like a tennis ball. I'm going closer, to 10^{-14}."

"Take your time!" says Prof. Parton. "Each step you take is a breakthrough for the Shrinkatron."

"You're doing *great*!" calls Max. "Keep going!"

This time you feel like a giant hiccup is passing through you. You are floating next to a huge reddish planet. *The proton!*

The next step is to get inside. You push

40

against the surface of the particle and carom away. It feels as if you are jumping on a trampoline, or running into a rubbery wall.

"Come in, come in!" squawks your wrist monitor. "Are you okay?" It's Max.

"I'm fine," you say. "I'm right next to the nucleus. But I can't push my way inside!"

"Maybe this is the time to test the power booster," says Max. "What do you think, Professor?"

"If you could push your way inside, you might be the first to find the particles we have been searching for," says Prof. Parton. *"Quarks."*

Suddenly your wrist monitor starts flashing a bright red. A siren is going off in the lab!

"What's going on?" you shout.

"It must be the intruder!" yells Max. "Something has gotten into the accelerator!"

"I want you to stay where you are," says Prof. Parton. "It might be dangerous to come back here. You are very close to finishing your assignment. I will go check on the accelerator while Max talks you through the experiment with the power booster."

"You can look for a quark anytime, now that we know the Shrinkatron works," says Max. "How about growing back to your normal size as fast as possible so we can send you into the accelerator? I have a feeling that the guy who stole my other belt is in there — and who knows what he's after!"

"I'll leave the decision to you," says Prof. Parton. "But be careful! Rapid growth could be very dangerous, and it's never been tried."

■ *Do you want to try to penetrate the proton? Turn to page 67.*

■ *Do you want to grow back to the lab? Turn to page 31.*

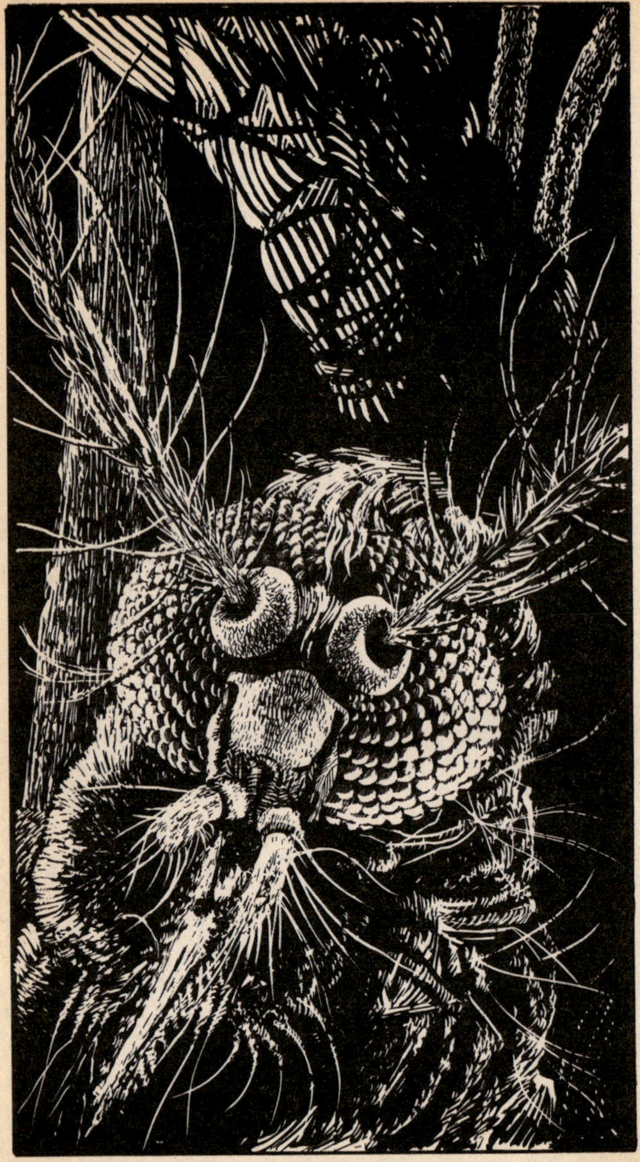

43

The mosquito lands next to the mushroom and stares at you with bulging eyes. Can it smell your blood?

You decide to battle the mosquito before you shrink any further.

The insect extends its razor-sharp proboscis as if it were a huge hypodermic needle. You watch in horror as it inches toward you. You always thought mosquitoes had delicate, spindly legs, but at this close range they look thick and hairy.

You circle the giant mushroom. Mushrooms don't have very strong roots, you remember. If you time things just right, you should be able to push...

The mosquito lunges. You hurtle yourself against the spongy mushroom and shove with all your might. It topples!

The mosquito buzzes angrily, then falls silent as it is trapped beneath the fallen fungus. The crushed cap of the felled mushroom gives off an earthy smell, and the dirt rustles at the foot of its uprooted stem. There's something there!

44

You move closer to investigate. Suddenly you are gripped by giant mandibles! Your arms are pinned to your sides and you can't reach your Shrinkatron belt!

It seems you have disturbed a very large ant. And four or five of his friends. For once, the ants will have a picnic all to themselves!

THE END

At 10^{-3}, you're one millimeter tall — 1/25 of an inch. And you are now faced with a mosquito that is as big as a two-story house!

You've never liked mosquitoes very much, but at this size, they are hideous, hairy, and terrifying! The insect is making a noise like a thousand chain saws and its quivering proboscis looks as sharp as a sword.

"Don't worry about that mosquito," Max's voice squawks on your wrist monitor. "You're too small now for it to take much interest."

"All the same, I'm going to shrink a size smaller," you tell your teammates. "I'm not ready to become anything's dinner!"

With a flick of the dial, you shrink to 10^{-4} meters. At last, you feel you have really entered the microworld!

"I can't tell what anything is," you say to the lab. "All I see are shapes — like circles and scales. I'm going to shrink again."

46

"Wait!" calls Prof. Parton. "We haven't tested two jumps so close together — what if..."

But you have already pushed the red button and felt the familiar shiver. You are 10^{-5} meters tall.

"Are you okay?" yells Max. "Ten microns tall! We've never been down that far before!"

"I'm fine," you answer. "Just give me a minute to get used to it!"

You're not sure where you are, but you feel as if you are floating. The unfamiliar shapes around you are moving and pulsing in slow motion. You are in a world of dreams, with no people, no streets, no houses, or furniture.

A squiggly creature whisks by you, its slender tail thrashing wildly. The force of its movement pushes you gently away, and you almost bump into a jellylike oval. The jelly is transparent, and you see bits and pieces of darker material floating inside it. As you look, the jelly stretches and splits into two identical parts.

You swim on, and drift by a cluster of particles, like bubbles or bits of dust. Suddenly a gelatinous glob narrows and flows around them. When the glob gels back to its original shape, the particles are gone. You look closer at the glob, and

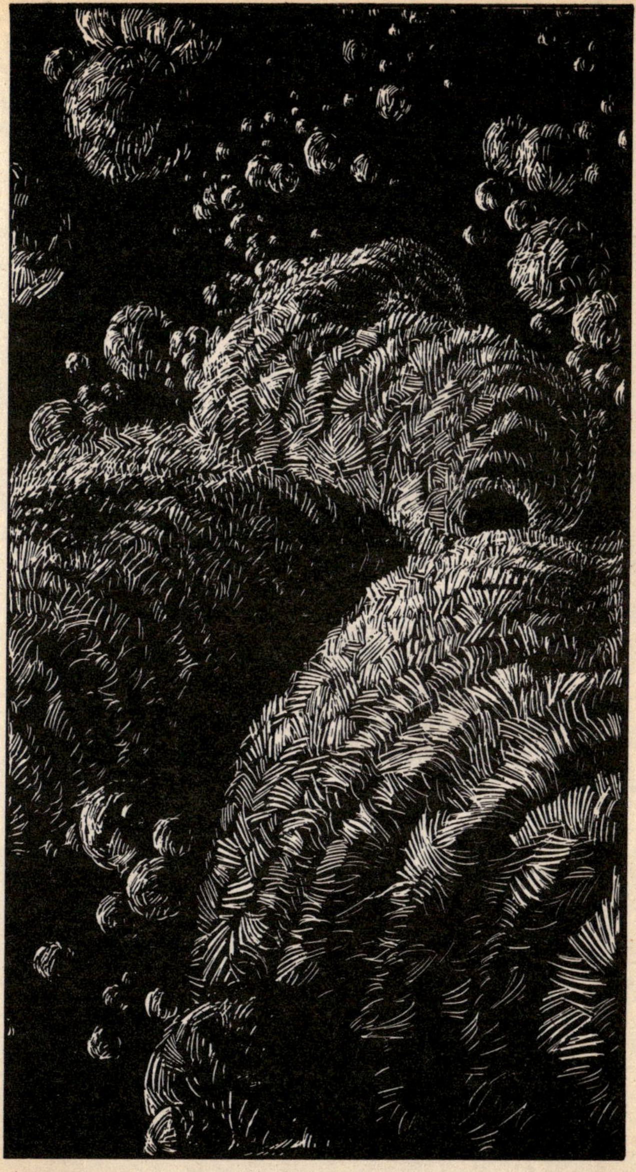

48

think you see some dark specks within it. Perhaps they are the particles.

Where are you, anyway? And could those tiny particles have been atoms? You see another cluster floating your way.

- *Do you want to investigate the particle cluster? Turn to page 51.*

- *Do you want to wait and check in with the lab? Turn to page 55.*

You move the dial on the Shrinkatron and work your way to 10^{-9}. You are feeling a little giddy.

"Are you okay?" Max asks from the lab. His voice sounds far away.

"I'm A-okay," you answer. "Just a little light-headed. Prof. Parton was right. I can see roundish shapes that must be water molecules. They're all clustered together. But I can crawl around between them. They look sort of like thin silk pillowcases with lumps of stuffing inside."

"Look closer at the lumps," says Prof. Parton. "Those are the atoms that make up the molecule."

"I'm floating next to one now," you say. "The molecule seems to have three parts. From here they feel like balloons. One part seems denser than the other two. The other two look alike and are joined to the first one."

"The single one is an oxygen atom and

the other two are hydrogen," Prof. Parton says.

"Great!" you say. "I'm heading for an atom. I'm going to shrink to 10^{-11}."

■ *Do you want to choose the oxygen atom? Turn to page 53.*

■ *Or one of the hydrogen atoms? Turn to page 63.*

51

You swim toward the floating particles. Maybe they are atoms. If they are, you could try to shrink and get inside one.

A large creature moves toward you. It is making slow progress. It advances by pushing a wobbly finger out of its body, then pouring the rest of its body into the finger.

It's not easy to travel in this liquid world. The cluster of particles seems to have broken apart. You draw closer. But a gelatinous glob is gaining on you!

You remember what happened the last time you saw a glob surround a group of particles. This time it looks ready to flow around you.

You have no desire to be gobbled by a glob. Pressing your arms and legs together like a champion diver, you wriggle away like a fish. You are bumped by a jellylike oval. Then another.

You are trapped between two jellylike ovals. You can hardly breathe. One of the

52

ovals narrows and splits into two. Now you are trapped by three jellylike ovals!

"Where am I?" you shout into your wrist monitor. "Are these things atoms?"

But it's too late. A jellylike glob has flowed into your wrist monitor and another is clogging your Shrinkatron belt. In no time you are surrounded. The jellylike globs fuse with your skin. Luckily they can't digest you, but you look awful. Once back to your normal size, your life is miserable until your agent signs you to star in *Globs from Outer Space*. After *Glob VI*, your fortune is secure, and you move to Pango Pango.

THE END

Step by step, you shrink to 10^{-11} meters.

"Wow," you breathe softly. You have to catch your breath. You're not sure where you are, but it looks like outer space.

"You're at *subatom-size!*" Max's voice sounds as if it's coming from under water. "Are you okay?" he is saying. "Where are you?"

"Maybe I've gone the wrong way," you answer nervously. "It's dark here, and there's lots of space all around me. It looks like it's filled with stars! There are bright, tiny sparks of light whizzing by in the distance, like comets. But they're moving so fast, I can't tell what they are."

"You've done it!" Max cries joyfully. "We've got a fix on your position now. You're inside an oxygen atom! Those lights are electrons!"

"But there are so many of them," you say. "The electrons are everywhere!"

"You're in an electron cloud," Max tells you. "What you are seeing is a pattern made by the electrons in motion as they dance around the atom's nucleus. But in an oxygen atom, there are really only eight electrons."

"They are beautiful," you say to Max. "I wish you were here to see them. It looks like a night sky. But what you are saying about electrons is not easy to understand. And where's the nucleus?"

"It's in there somewhere!" says Max. "And the electrons are just little whizzing bits of electrical charge. Maybe you could get closer to one. It would be like visiting a star!"

"It would also be a detour!" says Prof. Parton. "You won't find a quark in an electron. We need to find the atom's nucleus. Maybe you should try a hydrogen atom. Hydrogen is the simplest element, and its atoms have only one electron and one proton. It might be easier to find your way around."

■ *Do you want to head for a simpler atom? Turn to page 63.*

■ *Do you want to explore the electron cloud? Turn to page 57.*

55

"I'm surrounded by jellylike ovals and pulsing globs," you tell the lab. "There are some smaller particles, too. Are these things atoms?"

"Atoms!" says Prof. Parton. "You're not even close. Are the globs spinning, crawling, and swimming around you?"

"Yes," you answer.

"Are they splitting into identical parts?"

"Uh-huh."

"Are they flowing around the smaller particles and absorbing them as food?"

"That, too."

"It sounds to me like you are surrounded by single-celled organisms called protozoa. Amoebas, and so on. There are many different kinds. The big ones eat the little ones."

"Are they dangerous?" you ask.

"You'll be okay," says Prof. Parton. "You're in a droplet of water. But there are about a thousand billion billion atoms in a drop of water. You won't be able to really see one until you get to 10^{-9} or so.

56

"Then I'm ready to shrink again," you say. "I'll go as fast as I can."

"Take each step slowly," advises Prof. Parton. "Remember that we haven't tested the Shrinkatron to skip steps before. The next thing you'll be seeing at 10^{-9} is water molecules. Did you read your brief? If you didn't, Elwat will be happy to play it back for you. You won't reach the *inside* of an atom until 10^{-11}."

■ *Take it slowly and shrink to 10^{-9}. Turn to page 49.*

■ *Skip molecules and shrink right to atoms at 10^{-11}. Turn to page 53.*

You decide to explore the world of electrons. "Elwat," you say into your wrist monitor. "I need some data about electrons."

Elwat answers:

"ELECTRONS ARE ATTRACTED TO THE PROTONS IN AN ATOMIC NUCLEUS. THEY ARE HELD IN ORBITS AROUND THE PROTONS BY ELECTROMAGNETIC FORCE."

"Sort of like the planets of the solar system that are in orbit around the sun," you say.

"YES," Elwat responds. "BUT ELECTRON ORBITS ARE NOT AS SIMPLE TO PREDICT. THEY MAY BE CIRCULAR, OR ELLIPTICAL; THEY MAY TILT AT DIFFERENT ANGLES; THEY MAY BE CLOSER TO OR FARTHER FROM THE NUCLEUS; AND THE ELECTRON ITSELF MAY BE SPINNING. A TYPICAL ATOM MIGHT BE DIAGRAMMED LIKE THIS":

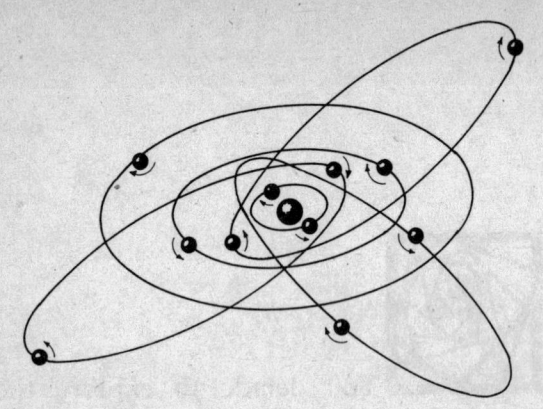

"No wonder it looks as though electrons are everywhere at once," you say. "Do you think I can catch one? Like a firefly?"

All three of your teammates answer you at once.

"Great idea!" says Max. "I could build you a charge adaptor, and we could capture one, like a proton...."

"No way!" says Prof. Parton. "The electromagnetic force that holds them in orbit is much too strong. I think you should move back to the hydrogen atom and continue your search for quarks."

"YOU'D HAVE TO FIND AN ELECTRON FIRST," says Elwat. "THERE'S MUCH MORE."

■ *Do you want to learn more about electron orbits? Turn to page 61.*

■ *Do you want to retreat to the hydrogen atom? Turn to page 63.*

You can't wait to try out your power booster.

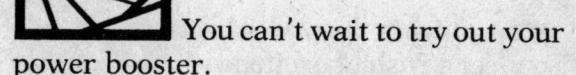

"Just how far away are they?" you ask Elwat.

"YOU ARE SOMEWHERE BETWEEN THE NUCLEUS OF THE OXYGEN ATOM AND ITS CLOSEST ELECTRONS," says the computer.

"LET'S SAY THE NUCLEUS IS THE SIZE OF A BOWLING BALL. THAT WOULD MAKE THE ELECTRONS ABOUT THE SIZE OF PEAS. AND THE ATOM WOULD BE ABOUT 20 MILES WIDE.

"IN OTHER WORDS, IF YOU WERE STANDING SOMEWHERE IN A SMALL CITY, YOU WOULD BE TRYING TO FIND SOME PEAS THAT ARE SCATTERED AROUND FOR 20 MILES."

"I could try to move the equivalent of twenty miles with the power booster," you say. "Would that bring me closer to an electron?"

Prof. Parton breaks in. "I think you are wasting your time," she says.

"It's worth a try!" says Max. "Let's go for it. But make sure you have it set for positive gravity, unless you want to end up out of this world."

"I'll be careful," you say. "I'm getting ready to hit the booster button. Here goes!"

You activate the power booster. *Vrooom!* You feel a rush of excitement, as if you've just won a race. The electron cloud swirls lazily around you. Then it stops and all looks as it did before.

You have to fight a wave of disappointment.

"I'm not any closer to an electron," you say into your wrist monitor.

"Our instruments show that the booster worked," says Max. He sounds confused.

"Even with the power booster, you were moving slowly compared to the electrons," says Prof. Parton. "But it's not likely you could ever catch one. Let me explain."

■ *Listen to Prof. Parton. Turn to page 65.*

"Okay, Elwat," you say. "Tell me more."

"WHEN ATOMS BOND TOGETHER TO FORM A MOLECULE, THEY SHARE ELECTRONS," says the computer. "A WATER MOLECULE LOOKS LIKE THIS":

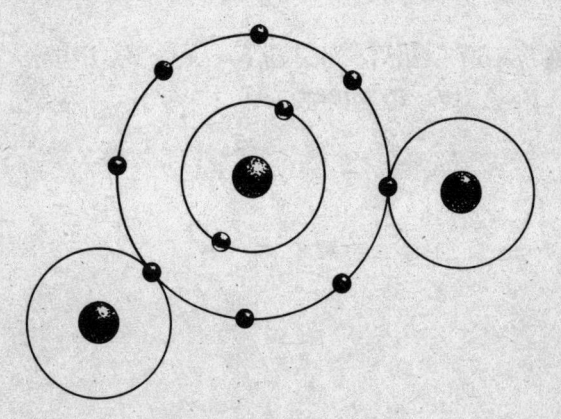

"I see," you say. "So if I could just harness one of the shared electrons, I could catch a ride into the hydrogen atom from here!"

"THERE ARE SEVERAL REASONS THAT WOULD BE VERY DIFFICULT," says Elwat. "FOR ONE THING, THOSE ELECTRONS ARE VERY FAR AWAY FROM YOU."

"No problem," you reply. "I could try out my power booster. Maybe if I get going very fast —"

"Great idea!" interrupts Max. "We haven't tested the power booster yet."

"ANOTHER REASON IS THAT ELECTRONS ARE HARD TO PIN DOWN. I CAN ELABORATE IF YOU WISH."

■ *If you want to try to reach an electron with your power booster, turn to page 59.*

■ *If you want to find out more about them first, turn to page 65.*

You are inside a hydrogen atom at 10^{-11} meters. All is silent.

"Boy, oh boy," you whisper, looking around. "It sure is dark and empty in here. I can see some sparks of light in the distance that look like twinkling stars. And it's kind of misty. But I'm just floating in space. I don't see any nucleus or anything."

"The sparks of light you see are made by a single electron," says Prof. Parton. "Its movement has created a cloud of electrical charge that looks to you like a sphere of mist."

"All atoms are mostly empty space," adds Max. "You might think that matter is solid. But when you get to the size of the nucleus, at about 10^{-13}, that electron will be orbiting at the equivalent of about ten miles away!"

"Then what makes things solid?" you ask. "Why can't I just walk through a wall like a ghost, if there's so much space between particles?"

"The invisible forces that act between the particles are too strong," answers Prof. Parton. "You can't push your body's atoms through the force fields in the atoms that make up the wall."

"Don't you remember reading about electromagnetic force and the strong nuclear force in your brief?" asks Max. "They are much stronger than gravity. But gravity has no importance in the microworld. Only large, uncharged objects, like planets and people and mosquitoes, are subject to the force of gravity. Are you ready to keep shrinking? There must be a nucleus in there somewhere!"

"I'm on my way!" you answer. Here comes 10^{-12}."

■ *Shrink to 10^{-12}. Turn to page 39.*

"I can tell you why you could probably never catch an electron," says Prof. Parton. "Sometimes electrons move from one orbit to another, or from one atom to another. We have no way to predict exactly where a particular electron will be at a particular moment. Even with the power booster, there is no reason to think that you would land in the same spot as an electron. And even if you did, as soon as you got there it would be gone."

"AT 10^{-11} METERS," adds Elwat, "YOU ARE MUCH LARGER THAN AN ELECTRON. IN FACT, YOU'RE STILL MUCH LARGER THAN THE NUCLEUS OF AN ATOM."

"I think it's time to get this experiment back on track," says Prof. Parton. "The particles we want to study are *inside* the nucleus.

"The simplest nucleus to study is the nucleus of the hydrogen atom, because it has only one proton. So I suggest you get back to the water molecule and choose one of the hydrogen atoms to explore."

"We'll use the power booster later," says Max, "when you try to penetrate a proton."

"Okay," you answer. "Quarks, here I come!"

■ *Head for the hydrogen. Turn to page 63.*

You've come this far. You decide to try to penetrate the proton.

"I'm going to try the power booster," you tell your teammates. "But first, I'm going to explore this particle a bit. That should give Professor Parton time to check on the accelerator."

You begin to circle around the rubbery globe. At first it looks reddish. But then you see that it really has no color. Or every color. Its surface feels alive and constantly changing. In places it feels grainy, like a raspberry. A roundish, grainy water balloon.

You notice you've begun to think of the proton as some sort of soft, exotic fruit. You don't want to bruise it. But as you press against its sides, you can feel the outlines of three moving "pits."

"I'm not sure what's inside here," you report to the lab. "But three places seem to have some sort of energy, like the electricity you feel when you rub a balloon. And they're moving."

"The quarks!" says Max. He has to yell over the wailing alarm that is still sounding in the lab. "Try the booster!" he calls. "This is too exciting to delay. The guards are checking the accelerator, and Professor Parton is on her way back."

"Here I go, then," you say. "I'm pushing the button on the power booster.... NOW!"

You careen into the rubbery proton, roll across one curving arc of its side, and plummet into the empty space beyond the stubborn nucleus. Over and over you roll. From time to time you catch sight of a receding reddish fruit. Soon the proton is out of sight.

"What's the report?" Max asks anxiously.

"I'm somewhere between the proton and the electron cloud," you say, "and I'm not sure I could find my way back. It's like outer space in here. I can't see anything at all anymore."

"I guess the power booster can't give you enough energy to penetrate a proton," says Max. "Not when you're standing still, anyway. But I'd like to see what would happen if you were already moving at a high speed — inside the accelerator, for example!"

"I can take a hint!" you laugh. "I'm on my way back."

■ *Head for the lab. Start to return to your normal size. Turn to page 31.*

You decide the risk is worth taking if you come back with evidence of a quark.

"I've always wanted to be a hero, Max," you say to the tiny video on your wrist monitor. "I'm going to try something." Then, slowly, you start to shrink.

Everything looks the same. It is pitch-dark. There are stars. The Earth is a tiny speck in the distance. Or is it the Earth?

"Max," you say. "Are you there?"

But your wrist monitor is crowded with dim, wiggly lines. All you can hear is static. You must be out of range for monitor contact.

Fighting a wave of panic, you decide you'd better grow back to where you were. Maybe this hero business wasn't such a good idea.

But the dial on the Shrinkatron is spinning out of control! You hit the power booster. The Earth disappears! You forgot to change the gravity setting!

"Are you *there*, Max?" you yell.

70

There is no answer. Your wrist monitor sputters and dies.

It seems you are lost in the infinity of space. But don't worry — the Earth must be out there somewhere. Maybe you can hitch a ride back on a passing comet!

THE END

It would be nice to be a hero. But your situation is risky as it is. Following Max's orders, you switch the power booster to positive gravity, then hit the power button.

The Earth draws slowly closer. You can see swirling clouds moving over huge land masses. You can just make out a shape beneath the clouds that looks like North America.

"So far, so good," you tell Max.

Now you are sure it's North America. You can even see your home state. You breathe a sigh of relief.

You can see mountains, and the lights of a city. It must be nighttime on earth. You've had a long day!

There's the accelerator! The huge, circular mound looks much as it did when you landed in the helicopter!

The laboratory building is right beneath you! You're over the roof!

You land gracefully next to the terrarium in the lab. The siren has stopped and

72

Prof. Parton hurries into the room just as Max gives you a big hug.

Prof. Parton glares at Max. "I seem to have missed something," she says. Then her face relaxes, and she shrugs her shoulders. "Just don't ever tell me what it was!"

She turns to you with a worried smile. "I'm glad you're back. Now let's get down to business! Are you ready to shrink again? The intruder has gotten into the accelerator! We're all in great danger!"

■ *Get ready to enter the accelerator. Turn to page 81.*

73

You set the charge adaptor switch for POSITIVE as a new burst of protons tumbles into the accelerator tube.

You are just one of the crowd as the protons jostle and push against one another. It's like being on a train at rush hour. But some of your fellow travelers are crowded so close together they interpenetrate!

"Are you okay in there?" asks Max. "You should be moving — we've activated the magnets."

"I'm A-okay," you answer. "I can't tell if we're moving, though. I'm surrounded by particles, and we seem to be vibrating slightly. But I can't see out of this dark tunnel. You didn't put any windows in here."

"I guess we never thought of that," Max says. "Take my word for it, you're moving. But the other protons shouldn't look to you like they're moving much. Imagine you're all riding in a car together. The other passengers in the car look like they're sitting still, because you are all moving at the same rate."

"It's more like a train than a car in here," you say. "It's jammed!"

Your "particle train" hurtles through the circular tunnel, gaining in speed with every circuit. You are getting used to your silent, spherical companions.

"Soon you'll be coming to another round of magnets," Max says. "Then you'll *really* be moving. You're already going incredibly fast. By the time you are ready to hit the target, you'll have traveled around in circles as far as it is to the moon and back!"

But you are hardly listening. Slowly pushing toward you through the jiggling group of protons is a dark, strange-looking particle. It has four tentacles, sort of like arms and legs. Arms and legs? *The intruder!*

The mysterious figure is still wearing a hoodlike mask, and you can't see his face. But around his waist you can see the glint of the stolen Shrinkatron belt.

"He's here," you whisper into your wrist monitor. "And he's coming closer! What should I do?"

"Can you see his belt?" asks Max.

"He has everything that I have," you answer. "But he also has a silver box with one switch and the initials 'QR' on it. What's that?"

"Quark Rectifier?" suggests Prof. Parton.

"Quirk Regulator?" says Max.

Suddenly your teammates face each other with looks of dawning horror.

"Oh, no," breathes Prof. Parton softly.

"A quantum reverser," whispers Max. "Just what we were afraid of. Whatever you do, don't let him collide with you. If he manages to reverse his quantum qualities, he'll be your exact antiparticle."

"You mean he can't explode if he collides with a proton?" you ask.

"No," says Max. "He's not a particle, he's a person. If he reverses his quantum qualities, he'll be an antiperson! The collision between your matter and his antimatter would blow up the lab. It could even blow up most of the state of—" ×#!#%#***ssquuuawk. Hummmmmm.

Wavy lines and buzzing static are all you can summon up on your wrist monitor. The intruder must be transmitting some kind of electronic interference. You are on your own in the microworld. And you are faced with a subatomic terrorist who seems to want to destroy the Quark Project.

The figure in black draws closer. He

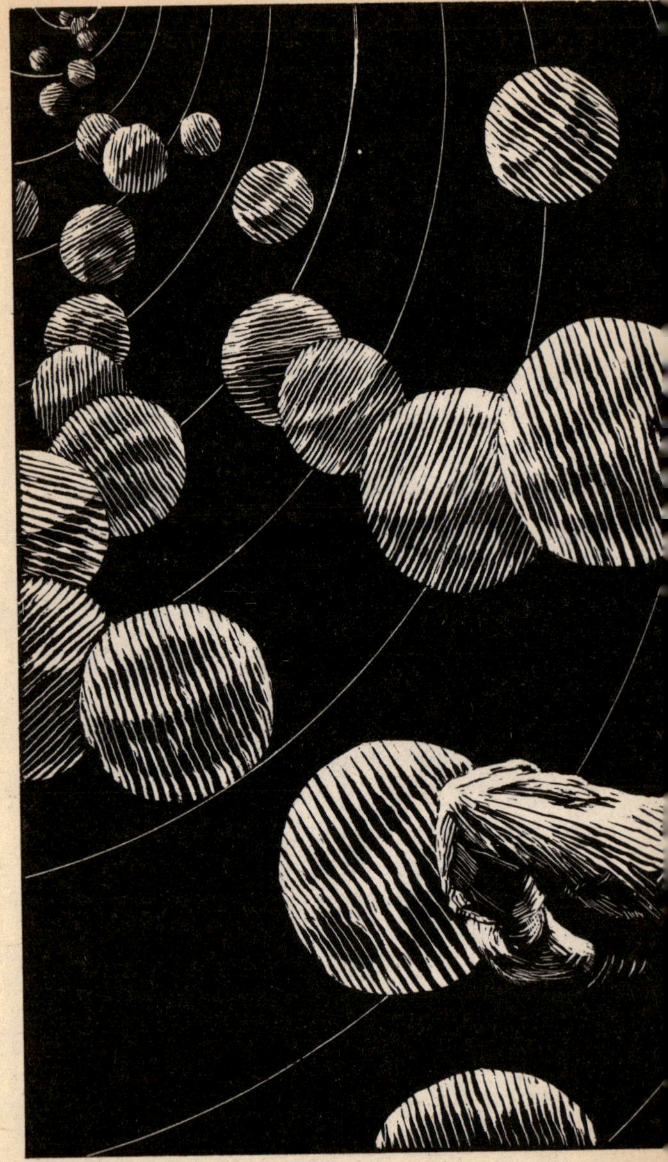

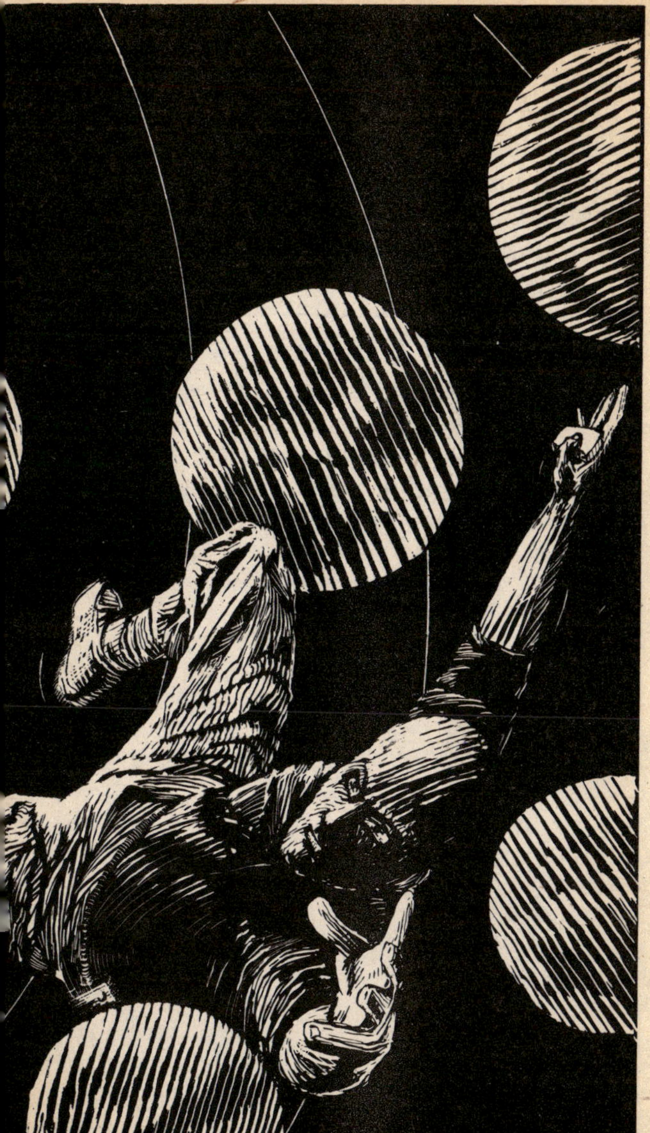

positions himself directly in front of you.

"How do you do?" he says. He laughs wickedly as his finger slips to the silver box on his belt.

All at once you understand his plan. You're on a collision course with a subnuclear nightmare! Act immediately!

■ *Do you want to use your power booster to blast past him? Turn to page 88.*

■ *Or do you want to put yourself in* NEUTRAL *and try to grab him? Turn to page 98.*

It's dark inside the accelerator tube. You continue to shrink until you are as tiny as a proton at 10^{-14}.

"All set," you tell the lab. "There's no sign of an intruder so far. Activate the proton beam."

A burst of protons fills the tube. It's like being in a tunnel filled with balloons or bouncing fruits. A second burst follows shortly thereafter. Then the particles start to move.

But you are left standing at the entrance to the tube. What's wrong?

You remember that the protons are reacting to the electromagnetic force from the magnets in the accelerator. You are still neutral, so the force isn't working on you!

You'll have to use your charge adaptor. But should you give yourself a positive charge? Then you could join the proton beam and travel along with the accelerating particles.

Or should you try a negative charge?

That way you would be attracted to a positively charged proton, just like an electron. If you got into a comfortable orbit, maybe you could hitch a ride with one of the protons.

■ *Choose a positive charge. Turn to page 73.*

■ *Select a negative charge. Turn to page 85.*

"What *sort* of danger?" you ask as you hurry behind the others toward the accelerator room. You're still only three feet tall, so you must run to keep up.

"We're not sure what the intruder wants," says Prof. Parton. "He may just want to be the first person to find a quark. But now that he is inside the accelerator, he could destroy us all!"

"We're afraid he may be searching for a way to harness antimatter," says Max. "You won't find antimatter anywhere on Earth — but you *will* find anti*particles* — inside the accelerator!"

"Whoah!" you say. "Antimatter? Antiparticles?"

"Every particle has its antiparticle, with the quantum numbers reversed," says Max. "They are identical, but all of their qualities are exactly opposite. If one particle has a positive charge, its antiparticle has an equal, but negative, charge. If the first particle is spinning slowly in one direction, its antiparticle is spinning at the same rate in the opposite direction. We describe these qualities with quantum numbers."

"So far, we don't know of any antiparticles combining to make atoms of antimatter," adds Prof. Parton.

"What would happen if they did?" you ask.

"When a particle meets its antiparticle, they annihilate each other in a burst of pure energy," says Max. "If there was so much as an atom of antimatter...."

"You mean the intruder could cause an explosion in the accelerator?" you ask.

Prof. Parton and Max look at each other and shake their heads.

"We hope that will never happen," says Max. "But you can prevent the possibility by capturing the intruder!"

"Maybe we can trap him," says Prof. Parton. "From the lab, we can control the proton beam in the accelerator. You could shrink to proton size and get him into a 'holding chamber' where he can't do any damage."

"And I have a new invention you can take with you!" says Max excitedly. "It's a charge adaptor. It will provide you with a positive or a negative charge. You will become subject to a new force of nature: You will be electromagnetic!"

Max looks envious as he fastens the little blue box to your Shrinkatron belt.

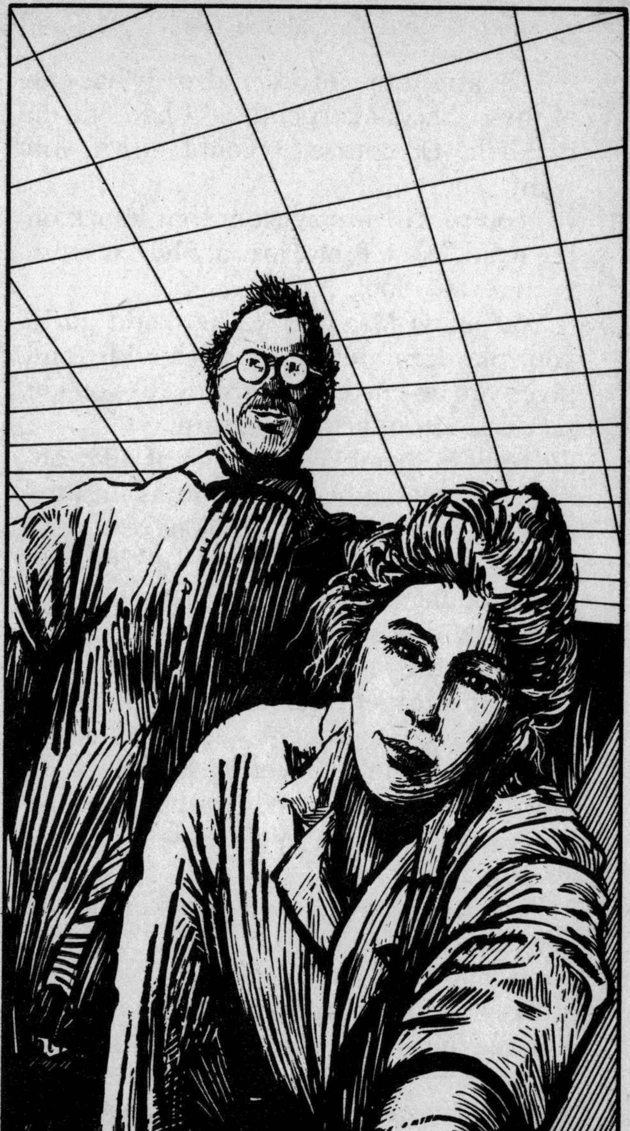

"I'm afraid the intruder already has one of these," he adds ruefully. "I had one on my belt. Of course, *I* could go, if you want."

"You're still woozy from that knock on the head," says Prof. Parton. She fixes him with a stern look.

You know Max wishes he could go in your place. But he pats your shoulder and gives you an encouraging smile as you get ready to start shrinking again.

"Now remember," says Prof. Parton. "We will send a beam of protons into the circular accelerator. Protons have a positive charge. As they travel around through the circular tube, they are given boosts of energy with a series of magnets.

"When they reach top speed, we direct them at a target made of other particles. The results of these high energy collisions are recorded in a detecting device called a bubble chamber. When the particles start colliding, you might have a chance to find a quark."

"I'm ready to go," you say, stepping to the accelerator. You step onto Prof. Parton's hand as you shrink to 10^{-1}. After your recent adventures in the microworld you feel *big* at only four inches tall!

■ *Enter the accelerator. Turn to page 79.*

You're eager to try out your new charge adaptor. You move the switch on the little blue box from NEUTRAL to NEGATIVE.

Suddenly you feel desperately incomplete. You are overwhelmed by an urge to grab the nearest proton. And the nearest proton seems equally attracted to you. How could you ever have thought that you could get through life without a proton of your own?

The charge adaptor must be working, you think, as you wrap your arms and legs around the sphere and clasp the grainy particle as best you can. You are filled with bliss. You are at one with the universe. Nothing else matters.

You barely notice that life is passing you by. Proton life, that is. All of the other protons are surging through the tunnel while you and your new friend stay behind.

"What's going on in there?" Prof. Parton's voice crackles over your wrist monitor.

"I thought I could ride along with a proton if I gave myself a negative charge," you say. "And now I'm happier than I've ever been. I've found my proton."

"You're not an electron, you're a person," barks Prof. Parton. "All you've succeeded in doing is combining opposite charges and making a neutral particle out of yourself."

"I know," you say. "It's wonderful — I think I'm in love!"

You can hear Prof. Parton talking to Max in the lab. "I *knew* something like this would happen," she says. "Did you build a remote control into that thing?"

"I never thought of that," says Max. He calls your name. "You have to *help* us! Uncharge yourself!"

But you don't take much notice. What could be more important than true love? And you know your proton loves you, too. That's why it's chosen you rather than anyone else — like that guy over there in the black ski mask, for instance.

You sigh with contentment. Love is bliss.

THE END

87

"I think it's time to call it quits," you say regretfully. "Besides, don't you think we should check on the intruder?"

"He's still in the holding chamber," says Max. He sounds disappointed, but he is trying to look brave. "Come on back, though. Grow very slowly."

You set the dial on the Shrinkatron for 10^{-14} and push the red button. The free-floating proton looks huge, big enough to walk around on.

"I'm going to 10^{-13}," you say. But then you pause. "Wait a minute — I've changed my mind. If I get trapped inside the proton, I'll just *grow* my way out!"

"Great idea!" says Max.

"That's the way!" shouts Prof. Parton. But you are already shrinking back to 10^{-15}

■ *Get ready to test the super power booster. Turn to page 96.*

You decide to use your power booster to blast past the mysterious intruder. But you may not be able to avoid a collision.

You hit the power booster!

Za-vooom! You feel as though you've been shot from a cannon! As you blast past the dark-hooded figure, you grab for the hand that is reaching for his belt. Your grip closes on clammy flesh. And cold metal.

Your scream of fear and determination fills the accelerator tunnel as you feel something tearing away. It sounds like a thousand strips of Velcro all being ripped at once. Is it your skin tearing loose? Is the lab blowing up? You speed into satiny darkness.

Ssscraawwk!##!$**. You are jolted back to consciousness by a horrible noise coming from your wrist. It's the lab!

There is a throbbing pain in your hand. You are holding something. You are squeezing it so tightly, your knuckles are white. It's a small silver box.

The quantum reverser!

You are still traveling with a stampede of speeding protons. And you must be getting near target acceleration. It's time to call the lab!

■ *Phone home. Turn to page 92.*

There's no time even to hold your breath. You smash into the target wall. But even as you hit, you can see that the pellet of frozen antifreeze is composed of thousands of atoms.

You remember that atoms are mostly empty space when you float through the first layer with ease. But next to you, an accelerated proton collides with the nucleus of one of the target atoms. Then you see another collision, and another.

You are surrounded by tiny sparks of light. Waves of energy brush past your face. They radiate in all directions.

Suddenly you're heading right for a proton! It's the stationary nucleus of one of the target atoms! You collide!

Your head is reeling as you spiral away through the dark space of the target. It's impossible to tell what direction you're headed in. But you have a feeling you've been knocked off course. Are you going the wrong way?

Your worry is answered as you find

yourself back in the loneliness of the accelerator tube. Another burst of accelerated protons is heading for the target — you have another chance.

This time you decide to use the power booster.

But what is that flailing shape in the distance?

■ *Use the power booster — quick! Turn to page 94.*

"I've got it!" you shout joyfully into your wrist monitor. "I've got the quantum reverser!"

Hummmmm. Ssquaawk##!$$# "... That's great!" Max is saying. Prof. Parton and Max come into focus on your monitor, and you have never been more relieved to see anyone in your life.

"But where is the intruder?" asks the professor. "Did you see his face?"

"He must be behind me in the accelerator somewhere," you answer. "But it's only a matter of time before he catches up. I still don't know who he is. But I have an idea!"

"Shoot," says Max. "We're all ears."

"You can control the proton beams from the lab, is that right?" you ask.

"You're on target so far," says Max.

"The target is the key," you say. "The target in the accelerator, that is. If I can beat this intruder to the target and pass through it into the bubble chamber, then you can redirect the proton beam behind me to one of your other holding chambers. That way *I* can keep looking for a quark, and *he* will be trapped!"

"What a great idea!" yells Max. "You're a genius!"

"I'll have to hurry," you say. "The intruder could catch up to me at any moment. Where is this target, anyway?"

"You'll see it as you approach," answers Max. "It's made of frozen antifreeze. It's thousands of atoms thick. When you hit, there'll be collisions between particles all over the place. Just try to keep going straight through to the bubble chamber."

"How much time have I got?"

"At least a few seconds," says Max. "This should be your last time around."

In the blink of an eye, a dense, gray wall rises before you. The target! You're going to hit! You, and all of the protons around you!

What if you're too solid? What if you can't get through? You begin to panic.

■ *Do you want to hit the target at the same speed as the protons? Turn to page 90.*

■ *Do you want to try your power booster? Turn to page 94.*

You check behind you. Sure enough, the unmistakable shape of the intruder is heading right for the target.

"Here I go!" you yell to your teammates. "As soon as I hit, redirect the proton beam into the holding chamber — the intruder is right behind me."

"The box! Give me my box!" he shrieks, reaching for you. His fingers brush the heel of your shoe as you dive for the target.

"NOW!" you scream. You hit your power booster and hurtle between the first layers of atoms in the target. Luckily, atoms are mostly empty space, and you do not hit anything.

You are whizzing past your companion protons. Many of the accelerated particles are colliding with the nuclei of the target atoms.

The darkness around you is filled with sparks of light. Waves of energy slap your face like rubbery winds.

Look out! You are headed for a collision with a nuclear particle. You can't tell if it's a proton or a neutron, but it isn't moving, and that means it's probably part of the target. Your only chance to miss it is to shrink again.

■ *Shrink to 10^{-15}. Turn to page 102.*

You are ready to test the super power booster.

"Slide open the little panel at the back of the power booster," Max tells you. "There's a button."

You find the button and position yourself against the free-floating proton. It seems to be pulsing. At 10^{-15}, the proton feels like a rubber bag full of cats!

"Here I go," you say, and *push!*

You can't see a thing. But you can *feel* something — a *tremendous* something.

"I'm in!" you tell your teammates. "I can't see any quarks. But I can feel them — they are moving, like waves. There are three of them — wait — I can see them some of the time. They seem to be spinning, and changing, and ... and maybe *exchanging* something, back and forth. I'm going to shrink one last time for a closer look."

You set the Shrinkatron for 10^{-16}.

"There's *another* particle here!" you say excitedly. "They are trading it back and forth. It's moving so quickly, I can't tell if there's one or many."

"GLUONS!" cries Prof. Parton joyfully. "You've found a *gluon* — the particle we think must exist to keep quarks together!"

Gluons? you think. Will the parade of particles ever end? But you are thrilled to have fathomed the depths of the microworld with such success.

Max and Prof. Parton are jubilant. You can hear them celebrating in the lab. On your wrist monitor you can see Max break out the bottle of champagne you know he has been saving for this occasion. Suddenly you feel lonely in this undulating rubber bag of cats. You want to share your exhilaration with your teammates.

"I'm heading back," you say into the wrist monitor. "Here I come."

You grow back to 10^{-15}. It's time to leave the proton and get back into the bubble chamber. You hit the super power booster. Nothing happens.

A wave of panic hits you like a water balloon. Are you stuck in the bag of quarks? Doomed to live as the only human in a world of uncaring particles?

Then you realize that all you have to do to break free of this rubbery cage is *grow*.

■ *You press the button on the Shrinkatron and grow back to your normal size. Turn to page 107.*

98

You decide to try to capture the intruder before he can do any damage. In an instant, you switch your charge adaptor to neutral and begin to slow down. He switches to neutral also!

No longer subject to the powerful electromagnetic force from the accelerator's magnets, you and the intruder are both losing your momentum. You are nearly bowled over in a parade of protons as the orbiting particles rumble past. Soon you are rolling and tumbling, unable to regain control of your own movements until the last of the protons stream by.

"I'll get you for this!" he screams.

As you are buffeted to one side you can see that the intruder is having the same problem. He has lost his balance!

Oooof! All at once you have the wind knocked out of you by a new stampede of particles. As you slow down, their speed increases! They are pushing you right toward the intruder!

The intruder reaches for the switch on

his little silver box. But an avalanche of protons knocks his hand out of the way.

You collide! Groping for the intruder's belt, you try to tear the quantum reverser away. You can feel the fatal switch, and press it back so it can't move.

The intruder is wrestling with your hand.

"Who are you?" you gasp at the masked figure. "What do you want?"

But the intruder is concentrating on the war between your hands. He is forcing your hand backward on the switch. You strain to hold your hand steady, and brace yourself for the next bombardment of protons. For the particles are returning on their orbit through the accelerator, and they are moving even faster!

Ka-voom! The protons hit, and your hand is jolted from the switch. In the same instant the intruder wrenches away from you and flies, spread-eagled, against a proton.

They are electromagnetically attracted, and firmly attached. You must have flipped the switch on the charge adaptor to negative. You weren't holding the quantum reverser at all!

The intruder is stuck to the proton like a pin on a magnet. Together, they become a neutral particle that bounces to a stop.

You approach cautiously and rip the mask from the intruder's face. You see a

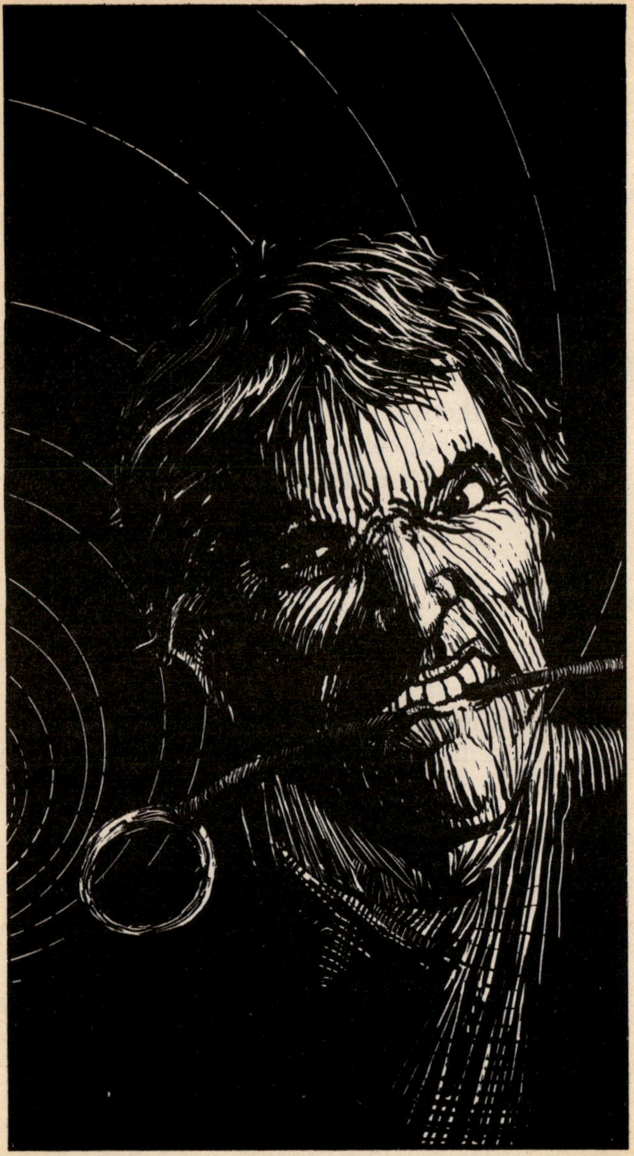

leering man with flaming red hair. And he's holding a rip cord between his teeth!

"Tell your friends in the lab that I can destroy us all," he says between gritted teeth. "This cord is attached to the switch on the quantum reverser. The slightest pull will blow us all sky high. Now, unbuckle your Shrinkatron belt."

You drop your Shrinkatron on the floor of the accelerator and yell into your wrist monitor.

"Max! Professor Parton! The protons — stop them!"

But you are too late. Another bombardment of protons is upon you. You barely have time to blink before the particles collide with the intruder and his head is yanked backward.

Ka-*boom!*

THE END

You hit the red button on the Shrinkatron. 10^{-15}!

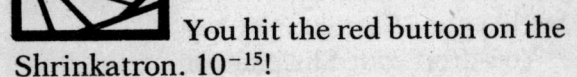

You miss colliding with the nucleus by a hair — even at these tiny distances — and plummet into a strange pool of liquid.

"I'm in!" you call to the lab. "I've made it through to the bubble chamber! Have you got him? Where's the intruder?"

"We got him!" says Prof. Parton. "We redirected the proton beam just in time. He's trapped in a holding chamber. Your idea worked!"

"Look at your monitor," says Max. "Here he is!"

You have to suppress a laugh. The angry intruder is thrashing about in a metal compartment like a fish in a fishbowl. As you watch, he shakes his fist.

"The guards are on their way. We'll deal with him later," says Prof. Parton. Her face comes back onto the monitor. "It's time to search for quarks! What do you see?"

At 10^{-15} you see particles colliding ev-

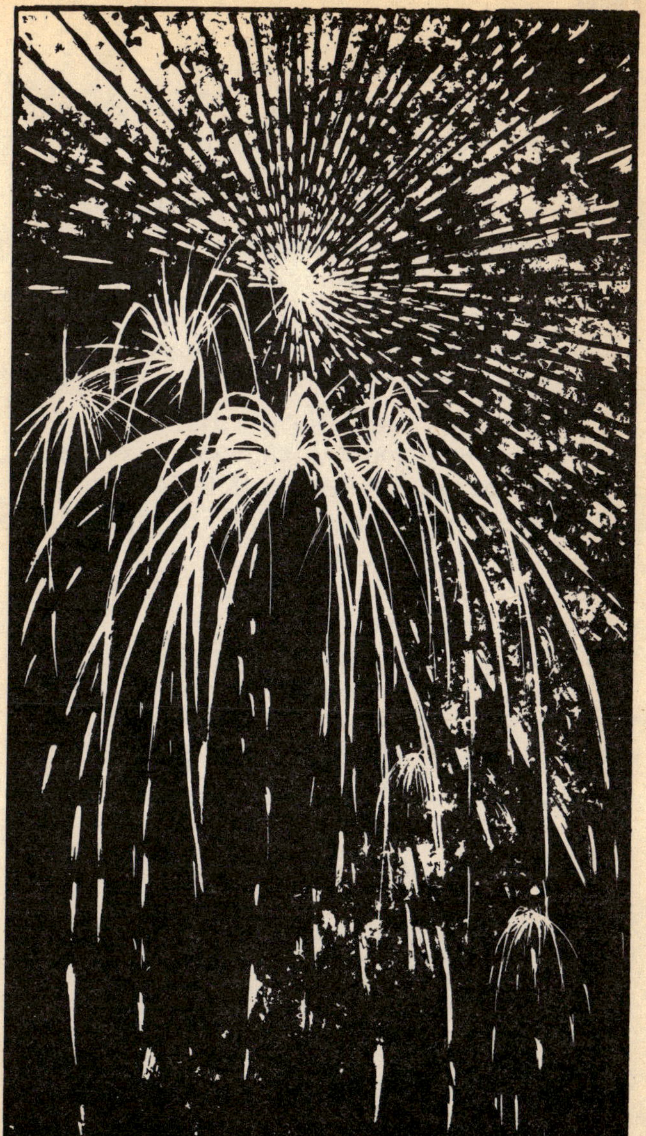

erywhere. They make bright flashes of light and spin away in every direction. They divide, split, bounce, spin, and whirl. They recombine and dance away. Some seem to disappear into little bursts of energy. Others cascade into streams of color like fireworks on the Fourth of July.

You describe them as best you can, but the sight is so wonderful it is hard to talk. The light show goes on and on.

"Some of the flashes of light you are seeing come from our cameras," explains Prof. Parton. "When particles collide at high energies, they decay into smaller particles. It sounds like you are seeing muons and pions and neutrinos and positron-electron pairs."

"What's a positron?" you ask, still enthralled by the fireworks.

"It's an electron's antiparticle," she answers. "An antielectron. But don't you see anything smaller? Perhaps something traveling in threes?"

"I don't think so," you answer. "But you just listed so many names of particles — how can I possibly remember all of those?"

Prof. Parton laughs. "Even physicists

need charts of the subnuclear particles we've discovered so far," she tells you. "Every time we turn around, someone has discovered a new one. Some of them just have Greek letters instead of names. There are well over one hundred of them now — we call it the subnuclear zoo!"

A familiar shape floats by you, and gives you an idea. "Didn't you say that particle physicists think protons are made up of quarks?"

"Yes," answers the professor.

"Well, I see a free-floating proton. It must have flown through the target without colliding with anything else. How about returning to our original plan? I could try to penetrate the proton."

"That didn't work last time," says Prof. Parton. "You didn't have enough energy to get inside."

"You do have one more chance," Max breaks in. "There is a SUPER setting on your power booster. And at 10^{-15}, you are smaller than you were in the terrarium. What do you think?"

"I've come this far!" you reply. "It's certainly worth a try."

"There's only one hitch," says Max.

106

You and Prof. Parton both sigh. You wait for Max to explain the hitch.

"You can only use it once," says Max. "If you penetrate the proton, you may not be able to gather enough force to get out."

■ *Do you want to chance it? Turn to page 96.*

■ *Or do you want to back out and grow? Turn to page 87.*

"It worked!" Max shouts into your ear as he helps you climb free of the accelerator.

"HOORAY. HOORAY," prints Elwat.

"How can we ever thank you?" says Prof. Parton. She gives you a big hug. "I have never been so excited!"

"What an adventure!" you say. "But I just realized something. If I can grow to escape a dangerous situation — so can the intruder!"

Your teammates' mouths fall open.

"We were so busy celebrating your success, we forgot to check on him!" says Prof. Parton.

"Let's go!" says Max, running for the holding chamber.

Before you even reach the metal container, you can hear someone banging on its sides.

"Let me out!" he is yelling. "I'm stuck! The quantum reverser is set to explode. Only I can disarm it! If you don't set me free, I'll blow up your precious accelerator and every living thing for miles around!"

108

You realize with horror that you are still carrying the little silver box marked QR.

"Give it to me," says Max. Gently, you pass the box to your teammate.

"Be careful!" says Prof. Parton. "We could all be blown sky-high!"

Max places the box on Elwat's monitor. "Scan this, please, Elwat," he says.

"RECTANGULAR CONTAINER COMPOSED OF STEEL," prints Elwat.

"CONTENTS: COMPUTER CHIPS; MINIATURE LITHIUM CELLS; ELECTRONIC SWITCHING DEVICE. CAPACITIES: QUANTUM REVERSAL UNDER CONTROLLED CONDITIONS. ZERO GRAVITY REQUIRED. NO EXPLOSIVE POTENTIAL AT PRESENT DIMENSIONS. TO NEUTRALIZE ENTIRELY: DISMANTLE SWITCH AND REMOVE POWER CELLS."

"The intruder is lying," says Max. "We're in no danger. The quantum reverser will only work when it is reduced to microsize, where the force of gravity has no meaning. But we'll destroy it, just to make sure."

Max yanks the top off the steel box.

"Look out!" yells Prof. Parton, hitting the floor. There is no explosion. Max pulls the switch loose from its casing, then dumps two round metal disks into his hand.

"The power cells!" he says.

"What are they?" you ask. "Miniature bombs?"

"They're the batteries!" laughs Max, as a troop of guards marches into the room.

"Remove the intruder from the holding chamber!" Max orders. "Make sure he doesn't touch the Shrinkatron belt he's wearing!"

The guards pull the dark-garbed figure out of a hatch door in the holding chamber. The hood falls from his head, and you see a wild-eyed man with flaming red hair. He snarls at the guards as they slap him in handcuffs and return the Shrinkatron belt to Max.

"You've foiled the greatest plot in history," growls the red-haired man. He narrows his eyes at you. "I could have ruled the world!"

"But capturing a Shrinkatron was central to your plot, wasn't it?" demands Prof. Parton. "How did you plan to use the quantum reverser, once you had a way to overcome the force of gravity?"

"I was heading straight for the White House," snaps the intruder. "With the Shrinkatron belt, I had a foolproof way to sneak into any building in the world. No one would have seen me. I could have planted a microscopic quantum reverser anywhere, set the remote control, slipped

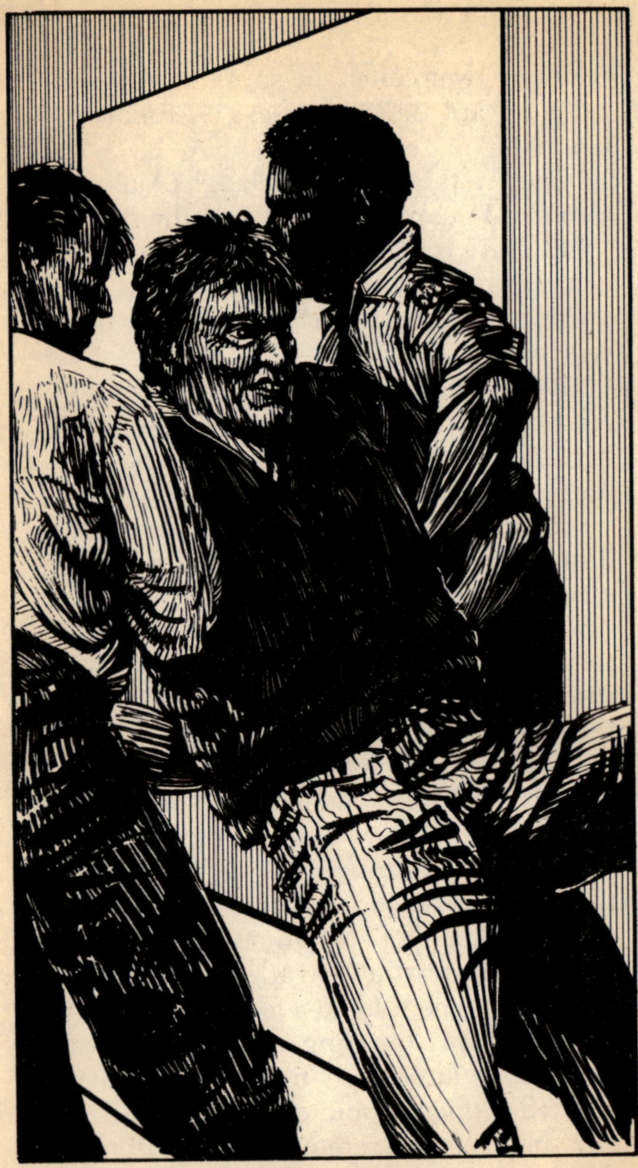

out the same way I entered, and then — *kaboom!* Think of it — the Eiffel Tower, the Kremlin, Big Ben! Humankind's greatest monuments, crumbling to dust! The world's leaders, quivering like jelly!"

The intruder's eyes are burning like little flames as he describes his victory. You decide you've heard enough from this mad terrorist.

"The air vent was your escape route from the lab!" you say accusingly. "But I spotted you, so you hid inside the accelerator. You planned to climb out on the far side of the ring, miles from the lab!"

"You are too smart for your own good!" says the intruder. The guards drag him away.

"The Pyramid of Cheops!" he wails. "The Great Wall of China!" His voice fades down the corridor.

"Well!" says Prof. Parton. "It seems you are a double hero today!" She beams at you proudly.

"And a true adventurer," adds Max. "You can borrow a Shrinkatron anytime you want!"

"CONGRATULATIONS. MISSION COMPLETED!" says Elwat.

THE END

TOP SECRET

The following brief contains information essential to a successful completion of your assignment.

1. Atoms are so tiny, they are hard for us to imagine: There are three or four billion atoms in the period at the end of this sentence.

2. There are over one hundred different kinds of atoms. Substances that are made of only one kind of atom are called elements. For example, the element iron is made of iron atoms.

3. Atoms bond together to form larger units called molecules. When a molecule is made up of more than one kind of atom, it is called a compound. A molecule of water, for example, is a compound of two hydrogen atoms and one oxygen atom.

4. The center of an atom is its nucleus. The nucleus is made up of two kinds of particles, the proton and the neutron. Protons and neutrons are sometimes called nuclear particles, or nucleons. A third type of particle, the electron, orbits the nu-

cleus — much like the planets of the solar system orbit the sun.

5. Atoms differ in the number of particles they contain. An atom of hydrogen, for example, has only one proton and one electron (the number of neutrons can vary), whereas an oxygen atom has eight protons and eight electrons.

6. Electrons are held in their orbits around the nucleus by electromagnetic force. This force is billions of times stronger than gravity. But it only affects particles that are electrically charged.

7. There are two types of electric charge: positive and negative. Electrons have a negative charge. Protons have a positive charge.

8. Particles of opposite charge attract each other. Particles with the same charge repel each other. Electrons are attracted to the protons in an atomic nucleus.

9. When the two types of electricity are present in equal amounts, a substance is said to be electrically neutral, or uncharged. Most matter — atoms, molecules, people, trees — is electrically neutral.

10. Neutrons are uncharged. They add mass to the atomic nucleus.

11. Protons and neutrons are held together by the "strong nuclear force." When we speak of nuclear energy, we are speaking of tapping a tiny fraction of the strong force. It is the greatest known force in the universe, 137 times stronger than electromagnetic force. But the strong force only works over a tiny range — the space between nuclear particles.

12. Nuclear particles can be broken down into subnuclear particles that cannot be seen even with the most powerful of microscopes. (Some of these particles have names — like muons, pions, and neutrinos — while others are identified by Greek letters.)

13. To find these particles, scientists use huge machines called *particle accelerators*. These machines generate the high energies needed to break apart atoms and nucleons.

The search continues for the most basic bit of matter, the building block from which everything is made. But the universe is like a set of Chinese boxes nestled one inside the other. Can you find the smallest box?

Scale of Universe in Meters

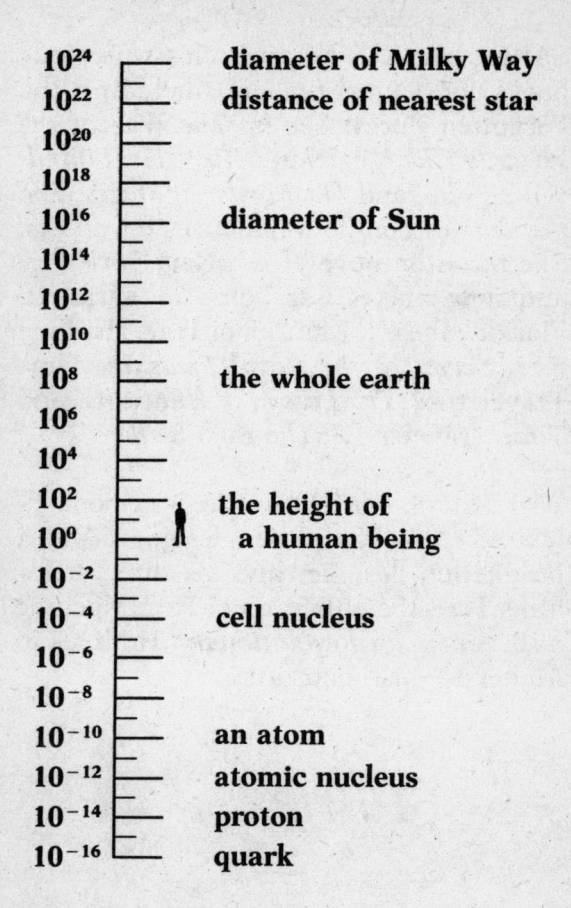

10^{24}	diameter of Milky Way
10^{22}	distance of nearest star
10^{20}	
10^{18}	
10^{16}	diameter of Sun
10^{14}	
10^{12}	
10^{10}	
10^{8}	the whole earth
10^{6}	
10^{4}	
10^{2}	the height of
10^{0}	a human being
10^{-2}	
10^{-4}	cell nucleus
10^{-6}	
10^{-8}	
10^{-10}	an atom
10^{-12}	atomic nucleus
10^{-14}	proton
10^{-16}	quark

END BRIEF.

■ *You are ready to return to your assignment. Turn to page 1.*

The Contributors

CAROL GASKIN has written six previous books for young readers, including the Forgotten Forest series: *The War of the Wizards, The Magician's Ring, The Forbidden Towers,* and *The Master of Mazes.* She also writes non-fiction articles for adults. She recently moved from New York City and now makes her home in Sarasota, Florida. She is the author of Time Machine #13, *Secret of the Royal Treasure,* Time Traveler #2, *The Legend of Hiawatha,* and Time Traveler #3, *The First Settlers.*

WALTER P. MARTISHIUS is a book illustrator, theatrical set designer, and a production designer and art director for films. He is the illustrator of Time Machine #10, *American Revolutionary.* He lives in Amherst, Massachusetts.